INNER-CITY SPORT:
WHO PLAYS, AND WHAT ARE THE BENEFITS?

The Authors

All the authors are from the University of Liverpool.

Kenneth Roberts is Professor of Sociology and Head of the Department of Sociology, Social Policy and Social Work Studies.

David A. Brodie is Professor and Head of the Department of Movement Science and Physical Education.

This research was funded by the Health Promotion Research Trust.

INNER-CITY SPORT

WHO PLAYS, AND WHAT ARE THE BENEFITS?

Kenneth Roberts and David A. Brodie

with Lucia Asturias, Rosie Campbell, Cherie Chadwick,
Sally Dench, K.L. Lamb, J.H. Minten and C. York

Stichting Uitgeverij Giordano Bruno 1992

Stichting Uitgeverij Giordano Bruno 1992

First published 1992 by
GIORDANO BRUNO CULEMBORG

Supplier's address
Hoofdstraat 130
3781 AJ Voorthuizen
The Netherlands
Tel: (0)3429-2097

ISBN 90 5013 018 6

Set by
Department of Youth, Family and Life-course
Faculty of Social Sciences
University of Utrecht

Cover-design
A. Koets
Beetsterzwaag

Printed by
Febo-druk, Enschede

CONTENTS

LIST OF TABLES

LIST OF FIGURES

PREFACE

This study is out of the ordinary in several respects. It is unusual, firstly, in the range of questions addressed: for example, who uses different types of sports facilities; what kinds of provision are most likely to attract different socio-demographic groups, what is the typical shape of lifetime careers in amateur participant sport, what are the relationships between sport participation and the rest of leisure, and the health and fitness implications of various leisure styles? Secondly, addressing all these questions involved unusually close collaboration between the natural and social sciences. Their contributions were not compartmentalised but intergrated throughout the research up to the writing of this book. For example, fitness testing was incorporated in survey work based on home interviews, and in the analysis and interpretation of the findings measurements of health and fitness have been treated like other social facts. The research was ambitious and took over four years to complete. It involved questioning over 7000 members of the public. Most of these were contacted initially during 1986 in user surveys at 46 sports centres in six different parts of the United Kingdom. Subsequently panels of participants and non-participants were followed-up over a two year period.

In addition to the subjects in the research, we are indebted to literally scores of organisations and individuals who made the study possible. We are grateful to the local authorities in the six research areas (Belfast, Camden, Cardiff, Chester, Glasgow and Liverpool), and to the managers and staff in the public, voluntary sector and commercial centres that we visited. We also wish to acknowledge the assistance of the fieldworkers who did most of our data collection, and the research staff who were responsible for much of the routine data processing. We are particularly grateful to Lorraine Campbell and Angela Sergeant for their splendid work throughout as project secretaries. Most of all, however, we must thank the trustees and staff of the Health Promotion Research Trust, and particularly the members of the project steering committee.

It was always intended that the results of this research should have practical applications, which is one reason why this book is written in a style that should make its arguments and their implications accessible to policy makers, sports providers and everyday players. Most of the detailed findings have been published as journal articles. Full details of the survey methods, response rates, and the structure of the data set are available from the Health Promotion Research Trust in a separate technical handbook.

While acknowledging the many sources of help without which the research would not have been possible, the authors alone accept full responsibility for the contents of the following chapters.

K. Roberts and D.A. Brodie

1

INTRODUCTION

Health and physical recreation

More of us are surviving into very old age than ever before, but this is only one of several reasons for health becoming an issue. We may be no less healthy in terms of our ability to grow old, but we seem more aware than formerly that our well-being depends not only upon access to high quality medicine but also upon our everyday diets, environments and lifestyles. This health consciousness is a reason for the switch to lead-free petrol, the spread of "no smoking" zones, the tightening of regulations governing food processing and distribution, and support for restrictions on even civil uses of nuclear power.

Coupling sport with health and fitness is relatively ancient. This has always been a justification for compulsory PE in schools and government subsidies for participant sport more generally. The Sports Council's long-running Sport for All campaign has always rested on the argument that physical recreation is not merely fun but also beneficial. In recent years the "sport for all" drive has meshed with the new health consciousness. The case for sport has been invigorated and, simultaneously, exposed to more searching scrutiny.

There is no dispute that sport players are generally healthier and fitter than citizens with more sedentary life-styles. Cause and effect are not easily disentangled, but hundreds of quasi-experimental studies have shown that sport training improves physiological functioning, and that regular exercise makes people healthier and fitter. However, it is not clear whether weekly swims, badminton or football games – the types of participation encountered in public sports centres rather than in training squads or experimental studies – involve sufficient exercise to confer health and fitness benefits. Also, although daily iron-pumpers undoubtedly improve their muscular strength, it is not self-evident that their general health benefits. Nor is it clear whether any health benefits from sport participation endure into later life-phases as opposed to being wiped-out once participation ends.

Given the aim of encouraging healthy living, what priority should be attached to physically active recreation? Are housing conditions, diet, alcohol and tobacco of greater or lesser importance? Are any types of sports especially beneficial for health promotion? And how frequently must different categories of people play to optimise their cost-benefits?

Promoting sport

In 1970 the United Kingdom had less than 20 purpose-built, public, indoor multi-sport centres outside education, whereas by the end of the 1980s there were over 1800. Sport participation had also risen, but not at anything resembling the rate of increase in provision. Despite the Sports Council's sustained advocacy of sport for all and the campaigns directed at target groups – families, the disabled, women, older citizens, the unemployed, and so on – most adults remained non-participants. Moreover, the relationships between participation and age, sex and socio-economic status were virtually as strong as ever. The modest rise in participation since the 1960s might have owed more to broader economic and social trends than to sport promotion and opening new facilities. The chances are that rising incomes, the spread of car ownership and the women's movement would have increased sport participation even if other things had remained equal. People with sufficient interest would probably have found somewhere to play if the new sport palaces had not been constructed.

By the early 1980s the Sports Council (1982) had moved beyond simply advocating and subsidising more facilities to cater for all-comers, and was setting targets for increased participation in specific age and sex groups, and urging local authorities to do likewise. Throughout the decade local government faced mounting pressure to obtain value for money in service provision. By the end of the 1980s the advent of compulsory competitive tendering for the management of sports facilities was imminent. Also, the Audit Commission (1989) had recommended that local authorities define their recreational aims clearly, assign money values to their objectives and select the most cost-effective methods or abandon all efforts if even the best strategies proved too expensive.

Up to now, following the Audit Commission's advice has involved more guesswork than science because so little is known about the kinds of provision and management that are most likely to spread physically active recreation among different sections of the public. Which types of centres, sports programmes, pricing, management styles and publicity, and what division of responsibilities between the public, voluntary and commercial sectors are most likely to deliver sport effectively to all sections of the population?

The study

Our research was composed of three strands which were designed so that their results would fit together and answer all the above questions.

i. Six cities

Firstly we studied provisions for indoor sport in six cities – Belfast, the London Borough of Camden, Cardiff, Chester, Glasgow and Liverpool. All are major UK cities. Five are the centres of large conurbations, the kind of settlement where the bulk of the country's population now lives. The research was spread across all the UK's constituent countries, but was designed specifically to investigate inner-city sport - what was available, and who was benefiting.

One reason for spreading the research across six cities was to compare the different policies and provisions of the local authorities, and the impact on the local populations' sporting lives. There were some sharp contrasts in what was provided, not always related to the local councils' current policies because in recreation, as in many other services, provisions had built-up incrementally over long periods. Some, but not all of the local authorities had embarked upon, or had recently completed major building programmes when our research commenced in 1986. Belfast's recent achievements were by far the most spectacular. Fourteen new purpose-built sport and leisure centres, all sited in areas of social and economic deprivation, had been opened between 1977 and 1984. At the other extreme, Camden could boast very few new works, while Glasgow's staple indoor sports facilities in the mid-1980s were still the baths and wash-houses that were opened in the late-nineteenth century. However, the large Bellahouston Centre had been opened in the late-1960s, and during our research the converted Kelvin Hall became an indoor sports facility and two leisure pools were built.

The councils also differed in the extent to which recent capital spending had been concentrated on large major centres as opposed to being thinly spread between community facilities. Here Glasgow with the Kelvin Hall, Bellahouston, and its leisure pools, and Chester with its impressive Northgate Arena but no other recent new-build projects, were at one extreme.

Another difference was in the extent to which the local councils were endeavouring to operate in partnership with the voluntary and commercial sectors. In some places, particularly Camden, collaboration with voluntary associations was a favoured strategy for maximising community involvement. Elsewhere, as with Chester City Council, limiting the authorities' own financial and management responsibilities had been a major consideration in the push towards "partnership". There was less "partnership" in Belfast and Liverpool than elsewhere, though for different reasons in these two cities. In Liverpool the Militant-influenced council of the mid-1980s had acted on an ideological preference for direct public provision. In Belfast, with its sectarian division, wholesale "partnership" was simply not a politically feasible option.

Another contrast was in the extent to which the local councils had adopted explicit social objectives and were targeting specific groups then monitoring the success of various programmes and centres. By the late-1980s

Camden and Glasgow were undoubtedly the most advanced in these particular respects.

Our research commenced in 1986 and continued until 1990, so we were able to monitor changes in the local authorities' policies, provisions, pricing and other management strategies, including their preparations for competitive tendering. The aim of this strand in the research was to assess what was available in each place so as to be able to investigate whether local provisions were making any difference to levels and types of sport participation among various sections of the local populations.

ii. Forty-six centres

The second strand in the research consisted of user surveys at 46 different indoor sports facilities in the six cities. These investigations were conducted in Autumn 1986. The centres were selected so as to cover as many types as possible ranging from large wet and dry facilities to church halls, and under public, voluntary and commercial management. Some of the buildings were old and shabby, whereas others were recently opened. In some centres the managements were simply managing the premises, whereas elsewhere there was more emphasis on marketing and targeting. The purpose of covering 46 centres was to discover whether particular kinds of buildings and management approaches, and whether public, voluntary and commercial provisions consistently tended to draw particular kinds of users.

In these facility surveys we confined our attention to users who were playing just seven selected sports – snooker, indoor bowls, soccer, badminton, swimming, keep-fit and weight training, and martial arts. One reason for concentrating on seven sports was to allow us to control the types of activity so as to see whether the types of centres and management, as opposed to the particular sports being offered, were making any consistent difference to the types of users. The seven sports were chosen so as to permit further comparisons. Two were relatively non-energetic (bowls and snooker). Among the more strenuous games, soccer and badminton represented essentially competitive sports that can be played only against an opponent. Swimming, martial arts and weights can also be competitive events, but these types of activity are more typically performed non-competitively, though sometimes still very seriously with a view to improving and maximising performance. We were interested in whether different types of sports attracted different kinds of players, and whether the effects of participation, especially as regards health and fitness, varied according to the type of game.

In each of the 46 centres we surveyed participants in the selected sports so as to obtain representative samples, which meant covering a large number of sessions and individuals. Altogether 7044 participants were encompassed. Of these, 1814 were children aged under 16, and they were simply counted. Out of the 5230 adults, 4554 (87 percent) agreed to complete a short questionnaire which sought information about each individual's age, sex, occupation if any, family circumstances, leisure behaviour, frequency of sport participation and use of any other facilities, means and length of journey to the centre being used when surveyed, plus six items through which assessments could be made of the players' health and fitness. Levels of non-response varied between the sports. The indoor soccer players had the highest refusal rate (27 percent). Participants in this sport typically arrived at their centres, changed and began to play immediately, and left almost as soon as their games finished. The participants in the other sports tended to be less hurried.

iii. Participants and non-participants
The third and final strand in the research involved follow-up investigations, primarily through home visits to 1387 of the adult subjects from the earlier user surveys, plus an additional 292 residents in the same areas who were not playing any sport regularly. The final question in the facility surveys was whether the subjects would be prepared to co-operate in later stages of the research, to which 83 percent answered positively and gave their names and addresses, and the individuals who were followed-up were selected from these volunteers. They were not a simple random sample from all the adult respondents in the user surveys. We followed-up equal numbers of men and women, from the middle and working classes, and from three age bands – 16-24, 25-34, and older. Also, as far as was possible within the above constraints, participants in the seven targeted sports and from each city were equally represented. The 292 additions to the "panel" were selected by quota so as to be distributed between the age-groups, sexes and social classes in the same proportions as the other respondents. Otherwise the extra subjects were simply representative of the local populations who were not active in sport at that time, and were added to the research in order to include an adequate number of non-participants.

The facility surveys were conducted in Autumn 1986, the initial follow-up was in Autumn 1987, and 1275 from this panel were also studied in the final phase of the research, a further set of home interviews in Autumn 1988. The majority of the subjects in this panel study were therefore questioned at three points in time, and most of the remainder on two occasions. The purpose of this multi-phase panel investigation was to collect more information than could be obtained in single interviews about each individual's biography, current lifestyle, and health and fitness, and also to measure changes over time. We gathered information about the sample's education, employment, family and leisure histories, about their current circumstances and lifestyles, particularly their leisure activities and any sport participation, and we also took a variety of measurements of health and fitness. One section of each home "interview" involved a set of simple physiological measurements – height, weight, blood pressure, grip strength, lung function, and flexibility.

A sub-sample from the main panel was invited to attend local sports centres where more extensive fitness testing was undertaken. In the 1987 fieldwork 372 individuals attended for these tests, of whom 244 were retested in 1988. Details of these fitness tests, together with the questions in the home interviews, are supplied in later chapters. The purpose of submitting a sub-sample to more searching tests than could be conducted in their homes was to learn more about the kinds of health and fitness indicated by the more limited home tests and interviews.

The panel contained enough individuals who were not currently playing any sport for comparisons with participants matched for age, sex and socio-economic status to clarify why the former had dropped-out (usually in youth or young adulthood) while the other's sport careers had been maintained. We studied a much larger number of current players than non-participants in sport because we did not expect sport to be uniform either in the reasons for people taking part, or in the consequences.

A danger in panel enquiries in which the same individuals are studied repeatedly is that there may be a "Hawthorne effect", meaning that the subjects' behaviour is affected by the study itself. In medical research this danger is routinely checked by administering placebos to control groups, but it is impossible to build equivalent safeguards into most social surveys. We were aware from the outset that repeated questioning about their sport behaviour and testing their health and fitness might prompt our panel members to re-assess and change their everyday lives. In the event, such effects did not appear widespread, as far as we can tell. The investigation certainly did not lead to most of the subjects playing more sport; later chapters explain that overall participation actually declined during the research. Also, a final set of questions in the concluding phase of the study asked if the respondents believed that the survey had made any difference, firstly, to their amounts of sport and exercise, and only 10 percent said that it had made some difference, with slightly more of these saying that the differ-ence had been "thinking about" rather than actually "taking" more exercise. A similar proportion, 11 percent, believed that the survey had prompted changes in some other aspect of their lives. Here the most common per-ceived effect was towards healthier eating. No-one can ever be absolutely certain, but we do not believe that much of the evidence that the panel supplied was artificially "manufactured" by the research.

There is just one major exception to this. Approximately 50 percent of the control group of non-participants who were first interviewed in 1987 reported in 1988 that they had begun to play at least one sport regularly during that year. This is an amazingly high figure. The resumption rate among lapsed adults in the general UK population is far lower. If a half of them tried to return, the facilities would be overwhelmed. Maybe the research had strengthened respondents' powers of recall when they were re-interviewed in 1988. It seems more likely, however, that our detailed questions about their health, fitness and sport participation prompted some to resume the latter activity. Testing which enhances people's health and fitness consciousness coupled with questions which raise their awareness of opportunities to engage in physically active recreation, and the knowledge that their health, fitness and lifestyles will be re-assessed in the near future could be an effective means of boosting adult sport participation. However, no such effects were apparent among the subjects who were already active in sport, and we suspect that our surveys did not change the entire course of many lives because other evidence from the research indicates that resumptions of sport careers following years of abstinence tended to be short-lived.

The prime purpose of the first strand in the study, the comparison of facilities in the six cities, was to establish exactly what was available in each area. The second strand, the facility surveys, was designed to discover who was using the provisions and the ways, if any, in which levels of use and the types of users depended on what was available locally. The third strand was designed to generate more information on why different kinds of people had dropped-out or remained active in different kinds of sport, and participated with different frequencies, and to assess the consequences, particularly for health and fitness.

The aim of the entire research programme was not to rediscover that sport participants tend to be young, male and middle class. The findings certainly confirm that this remained the case, in the late 1980s, but this was not the prime purpose of the exercise. Nor was the intention simply to develop better explanations of the social distribution of sport activity, though the findings do indeed clarify the processes that are responsible. The main objectives were to discover whether any politically and economically realistic changes in provision – in the types of facilities, pricing, management, location or whatever – were likely to raise levels of participation and reduce inequalities, and to establish the probable consequences, the costs and the benefits, the implications for well-being and the quality of life, especially in terms of health and fitness.

The results that are presented in the following chapters indicate beyond all reasonable doubt, in our view, that sport participation not only makes people healthier and fitter, but is associated with generally rich and active lifestyles and low levels of stress. Our evidence also suggests that appropriate provisions will accelerate the spread of such lifestyles. However, the evidence also warns that these effects of appropriate provisions will be fully realised not within months or even years, but only over decades and generations. This means that using sport to raise levels of public health and fitness, and thereby to achieve an overall improvement in the quality of life, should be treated as a long-term strategy. The project will be unattractive to anyone seeking quick returns. Our evidence also shows that there will be a price to pay for the benefits; namely, that the growth in provision for sport that has been achieved in the UK since the 1960s will have to continue into the twenty-first century. By then the new centres that were opened in the 1970s and 80s will be middle-aged. They will need to be supplemented, upgraded or replaced. Provisions will have to keep pace not only with the volume of demand, and also with the spiral of rising expectations that seems certain to accompany a long-term rise in sports interest and activity.

Chapters 2-6 deal with facilities and participants, and reach conclusions about the kinds of sport policies and provisions that will maximise participation in all age and sex groups, and social classes. Our analysis assumes the desirability of maximising sport participation and asks how this might be achieved, but this is not a case of a value judgement being introduced surreptitiously. It is introduced consciously and openly, not in order to make converts but purely for the purpose of presenting our evidence so as to answer a question that led to the research being undertaken. Temporarily we suspend final judgement and postpone discussion of whether more widespread sport participation really is desirable. The subsequent chapters contain the evidence that permits more informed discussion of this matter. They examine the consequences of sport participation for people's wellbeing, particularly the health and fitness benefits, and the costs also, for sports injuries are considered alongside improvements in physiological functioning. These chapters also delve into the broader lifestyles of sport players and non-participants and explain how, for the majority of the participants in this investigation, sport had become just one element in what were intended to be generally health promoting lifestyles.

2

PROVISIONS IN THE SIX CITIES

The six city councils had different histories of providing for their people's leisure. They also differed in their current priorities. So there were major differences in their levels and types of public sport provisions by the mid-1980s. However, the local authority was the main provider in each of the cities, and all were offering combinations of dual use (by education and the community) and straight-forward community facilities.

The voluntary sector was a force everywhere. It was always the main organiser of leagues, clubs and teams even when it did not own and manage the premises where they played. The prominence of the voluntary sector as a provider of actual facilities seemed to depend mainly on the local councils' policies – whether they favoured provision by grant-aiding voluntary bodies – and secondarily on the local presence or absence of voluntary organisations with sufficient resources to own and manage facilities. Long-established movements such as the YMCA, national sports federations, and some local sports clubs had the necessary finance and management capability, but such examples of voluntarism were not equally represented in all the cities. However, all the cities contained churches and other community groups with premises (rarely built for the purpose) that were wholly or part-used for sport.

The commercial sector was making much the same impact in each of the cities. It was operating numerous snooker clubs and health and fitness studios, some of which were independent establishments while others were based in hotels and larger entertainment complexes. One likely reason why the commercial sector was filling these niches everywhere was that other parts of the sport market were rendered non-profitable by heavily subsidised public and voluntary provisions. However, as explained in chapter six, commerce appeared to be adding an extra something that other types of centre were unable or unwilling to emulate.

Public facilities

The local authority was the main architect of each city's overall level and pattern of indoor sport provision. All six city councils were the main local providers of facilities, but exactly how much and what was provided varied considerably. Also, between 1986 and 1989 there were major changes in the levels and quality of provision in some, but not all of the cities. The councils had different histories of providing for physical recreation. Some had completed or were well into co-ordinated building projects which were leaving planned networks of purpose-built centres. Others had less tidy provisions which had been built or converted at different times for many different reasons. In some places recent developments had been based more on upgrading than opening entirely new centres. However, the problems that the leisure departments faced, and the solutions being adopted, were tending to converge in the late-1980s. New building was being dismissed as impractical unless it took the form of co-operative ventures with the commercial sector. All the leisure departments were looking for new ways of raising revenue in order to meet their costs, and were keen to upgrade facilities to keep pace with ever-changing tastes. The departments were rationalising existing provisions, preparing for the future leisure market, and also for compulsory competitive tendering (CCT).

Liverpool
In 1986 Liverpool's Parks and Recreation Department was guided by a plan produced in 1983. This outlined a strategy for city-wide new build projects and identified priority areas of need where new centres were to be sited. Assisted by an injection of central government resources following the 1981 disturbances, the city council had expanded its indoor sport provisions considerably. A network of SASH (Standardised Approach to Sports Halls) centres was being built on sites identified in the recreation plan. By 1986 there were four such centres plus one slightly older, but larger modern purpose-built indoor sports facility. Liverpool also had one major dual-use facility, two older wet and dry centres, another small dry centre and several older public baths. By 1989 two further SASH centres were open, one incorporating the city's first leisure pool. The Labour controlled council had preferred direct public provision to partnership, and had opted for the SASH package because these centres were quick to build and relatively cheap thereby enabling the city to be given a network of value-for-money community-based centres. There was only one major sports centre owned and run by a voluntary association in the city to which the council gave no support. Compared with our other cities, Liverpool was not particularly short of indoor sport provisions in 1986, and the city was even better-provided by 1989. Its looming problem was that only one of its centres could be described as a "high quality" asset.

Cardiff
Prior to 1978 there were no modern public indoor sports centres in Cardiff. Then the city council embarked upon a development programme which by 1986 was coming to a close leaving Cardiff with five large, modern, good quality wet and dry leisure centres scattered throughout the city. During the

course of our research another centre incorporating the city's first leisure pool was opened and a second leisure pool was added to an existing centre. Public provision in Cardiff also included a small converted sports centre, one large public pool, an international pool with a modern fitness centre and turkish baths, and four modern community halls with sports facilities. Public provision was extensive with an emphasis on large, modern, wet and dry multi-purpose buildings which incorporated facilities such as "high-tech" weights and conditioning rooms. Over the previous 10 years the council had invested £15 million in leisure provision, and in 1989 this spending seemed likely to continue with the proposed building of a further district leisure centre to complete the current construction plan.

Provision in Cardiff was complemented by the Sports Council managed National Sports Centre for Wales, as well as two voluntary trust run dry sports centres. These centres had been built in a co-operative venture between South Glamorgan County Council, Cardiff City Council and two charitable trusts which had managed the projects since their inception. The city council had donated the land on which to build the centres and had helped with design, planning and funding. Compared with Liverpool, Cardiff did not have "more", but, certainly in physical terms, its indoor sports facilities were of a higher standard.

Belfast
Between 1977 and 1984 Belfast City Council opened 14 new, purpose-built indoor leisure centres. So by 1986 Belfast had an impressive network of newly built centres which far surpassed in quantity and quality those found in most UK and European cities. It was far-and-away the best-provided of the cities that we studied. The leisure centres in 1986 were organised in a three tier structure. There were four first tier centres; all major wet and dry facilities. They were complemented by four second tier centres – somewhat smaller district-based facilities, and six third tier centres – still smaller dry neighbourhood buildings. Four swimming pools were also managed by the council.

By 1989 there were five second tier centres, one of the swimming pools having been upgraded. Residential accommodation had been added to this centre, and its pool was acting as the centre of excellence for swimming in Northern Ireland. By 1989 the Falls Road pool had also been upgraded and had replaced the Stadium Recreation Centre in the third tier. This centre was the only original tier three facility not to have been purpose-built, and was transferred to the voluntary sector during the course of our research. By 1989 it was being run as a youth centre by the Elim Pentecostal Church. The Leisure Services Department disbanded its pools section while our research was underway. One of the city's ageing pools was closed, and the sole remaining "traditional" pool was handed over for management by a local voluntary group. Other changes had taken place at individual centres in order to keep pace with modern leisure tastes. For example, a "high-tech" fitness facility had been introduced in one of the first tier centres.

Belfast's high level of public provision was the end-product of a unique history of leisure development in which the sectarian "troubles" had played a part. The "troubles" were not the reason why such centres were originally recommended (Roberts et al, 1989). Belfast in the late 1960s was just one of numerous UK cities that were planning a future with better leisure provisions than in the past. However, recommendations for an expansion of indoor leisure provisions were treated as urgent after the violent outbreaks between the catholic and protestant communities in 1969. Central government then released funds to support an extensive leisure centre building programme. Provision for sport and leisure was a relatively non-controversial means of attempting to improve the quality of life in the city. No-one believed leisure provision would solve Belfast's other problems. Rather, the intention was to improve the quality of life alongside or even in the absence of other economic and political initiatives.

Glasgow
In 1985 Glasgow adopted a recreation plan for the period up to 1995 which recognised "a major deficiency" in indoor sport provision. In 1986 the city's dry facilities consisted of three fairly modern centres, two smaller older centres, and one modern sports complex attached to a synthetic running track. There were also two small wet and dry centres, both upgraded nineteenth century bath houses. There were very few modern facilities in so large a city. Altogether there was a network of 14 recreation centres, but most were equipped to play only a minor role in sports provision. The city had several old swimming pools with high running costs and in need of upgrading. The council recognised that its priority up to the 1980s had been to house its people rather than to cater for their leisure.

The recreation plan outlined a development programme giving priority to upgrading selected pools. On the dry side, the plan envisaged retaining existing centres and using them as a springboard for additional facilities. There was a recognised need for new dry sports facilities, but within the confines of a limited budget. Glasgow was perhaps in the most difficult position of all the research areas in 1986. Unlike Cardiff, it was stuck with ageing facilities and limited resources which made an extensive new build programme unrealistic. However, a limited building programme was planned. Public provision was somewhat behind the times, and the city's poor quality centres were not attracting the public.

By 1989 Glasgow was in an improved position. One major development had been the re-opening of the Kelvin Hall in 1987. This impressive facility had become the city's premier site for community events as well as national and international sports fixtures. Two dry centres sited on Glasgow's peripheral estates, Easterhouse and Castlemilk, had been built using Urban Programme and Scottish Development Programme funding. These developments were in line with a policy of grouping together council facilities. The centres were built near existing pools, outdoor facilities and play areas. Although such recreation centres still played only a minor role in indoor sports provision, changes were in hand with plans to use them as feeders to the major sports facilities. One new SASH centre had been built, while some of the older centres had been improved and upgraded. The Pollock leisure pool had opened, the city's first of its kind. Govan pool had also been "leisurised" and five pools had undergone or were in the process of upgrading. One ongoing project involved a major renovation creating Roman style baths and a fitness suite. One pool had been closed and only two of Glasgow's sports centres and swimming pools remained in poor condition.

Camden

In 1986 public indoor sports provision in Camden was not extensive. Provision amounted to three large wet and dry sports centres and a refurbished Victorian baths. The development of leisure facilities had been based upon upgrading existing buildings. This was due to the constraints imposed by the cost and non-availability of land in central London. The expense of land on which to build in the capital was too great for the Recreation Department to contemplate new build projects. One option being considered in 1989 was the demolition and re-building of its largest centre at Swiss Cottage in co-operation with a commercial partner. In 1989 a modernisation programme was just beginning at Kentish Town Baths with the addition of a dance studio. Upgrading was also in process at the Oasis Centre in London's West End, while at Swiss Cottage a fitness suite was being added. The Armoury Sports Centre had become a financial liability to Camden. The department could not afford the investment necessary to reduce the running costs and increase throughput to the levels considered necessary to put the centre in shape for compulsory competitive tendering. In 1989 the centre was managed by a community trust which, in return for a rent paid to the council, kept any profits. The Labour controlled council had been resistant to projects with the private sector, but severe financial cuts in 1987 and a desire to remain involved in sports development had limited their options. In 1989 a major retail company was developing a community facility attached to a store which incorporated a sports hall, arts studio and creche. No final decisions had been made but it was possible that the sports centre would be run by a local management committee grant-aided by the local authority. This signalled a shift towards the council seeking partnership with other sectors.

Chester

Chester stood apart from the other cities having a much smaller population, a relatively small inner-city area, and a higher proportion of middle class residents. In 1986 provision was dominated by one impressive wet and dry facility in the city centre, the Northgate Arena. This remained the city's sole major facility in 1989. There were two smaller dry dual-use sports centres located in residential areas, but there were no significant changes in levels of provision during the research. At Northgate alterations had been carried-out to keep up with leisure trends: a new modern sauna suite and weights room had been created, and a flume added to the pool. At one of the dual-use centres there were plans to open the school pool to the public.

A significant change had been the creation of a Leisure Services Department in 1989 in order to deal with CCT. Chester must have been one of the last councils in the UK to form such a department. Although the level of provision in the city itself was modest, there were three large sports centres within a 10 mile radius. Also, the old Chester City Baths, which had been scheduled to close with the building of Northgate Arena, was instead handed over to a voluntary association which was continuing to manage the facility.

Types of centres

An obvious way to compare public indoor sports centres is by their size. Indeed, our cities' local authority departments usually categorised their facilities according to this yardstick. Belfast, for example, presented its centres in a three tier structure. Four of the other five cities also had centres that were officially regarded as *major* or *premier*, with Camden as the exception. This London Borough had no "prestige" public centre, though neighbouring authorities had such facilities. Centres considered "first tier", "premier" or "major" were invariably wet and dry, offered facilities for a wide range of sports, could accommodate spectators as well as players, were used for major regional events and, in some cases, for international fixtures. In addition to premier or major centres, some cities had "other main" facilities, and there were invariably smaller community or neighbourhood provisions. *Other main* centres would have at least one full-sized sports hall and often a swimming pool. The physical condition of centres in this group varied greatly. Some were purpose-built. Others were older buildings not used for sport in the past which had been converted and, sometimes, upgraded as well. All the cities had *smaller centres*, usually regarded as serving their local neighbourhoods. Some were purpose-built, whereas others were old but refurbished. *Dual-use facilities*, parts of schools and colleges normally available to "the community" only outside school and college hours, were often regarded as belonging in this category. The purpose-built neighbourhood centres had no pools, and their sports halls were less than full-sized. These and the dual-use facilities were invariably being managed with a view to serving the surrounding communities rather than drawing from city-wide catchment areas.

The modal pattern of historical development, in modern times, had been for the major "prestige" buildings and district centres to be built first, followed by in-filling community provisions. The latter development had often included the upgrading of traditional "baths" which had invariably suffered a decline in use once newer facilities became available. However, there were exceptions to this sequence, most notably in Glasgow where the Kelvin Hall was converted for sports use in the 1980s.

There was great diversity in voluntary provisions, so much as to make it misleading to refer to these facilities as if they were managed by a homogeneous or co-ordinated sector. The cities' voluntary provisions could be grouped according to their size and the variety of sports offered, like public centres. However, in the cities that we studied the type of voluntary organisation seemed to be as important in shaping each centre's character. Four main types of voluntary provider could be distinguished.

i. Sports associations

National and regional federations and governing bodies often own and manage independent facilities; playing fields, running tracks, and/or indoor provisions. Facilities owned and managed by national associations in the cities that we studied were not necessarily restricted to elite athletes. They were mostly available for some general community use. Indeed, grants from the local authorities were normally conditional on this access. In addition to facilities run by national sports associations, many local sports clubs also owned grounds and club houses which contained provisions for indoor sport. It was up to the clubs in question whether these facilities were open to non-members.

ii. Community groups

Prior to the mass construction of public sports centres, the church hall was a typical venue for badminton and other indoor games, and in the 1980s there were still numerous premises owned and managed by community groups with broader interests, and which were being used primarily for other purposes, but which were devoted to various sports at different times of the day and week.

iii. Youth organisations

Some of Britain's youth organisations have histories now spanning a century. During this time many have become property owners, sometimes on what are now prime city sites. These organisations were still very much alive, administering premises and erecting new buildings, many of which were wholly or part-used for sport in the cities that we investigated. The youth organisation most prominent in sports provision in these cities was the YMCA. Indeed, in four of the areas it was a major provider. Three of the facilities were "traditional" centres; old and in various stages of refurbishment. The fourth, located in Camden, was a modern complex incorporating sport, social, cultural and residential provisions. This centre operated the kind of membership system and charges normally associated with the commercial sector and, not surprisingly, had a rather different clientele than other YMCAs.

iv. Privatised

These facilities had been brought into existence and, in some cases, were continuing to exist only with the support of the public authorities. Some like

Chester City Baths were once owned and managed by the local authorities but had been handed to voluntary associations, sometimes with grants to help to cover the running costs. Others as in Cardiff had been built with public funds then handed immediately to existing or specially constituted voluntary management committees. Some of the local authorities in our research were enthusiastic privatisers. Their motives were a combination of wanting to promote genuine public participation in the management of facilities, and a desire to limit the authorities' own financial responsibilities. In some areas voluntarism was a policy of councils led by parties of the right. Some local authorities dominated by parties on the left considered direct public provision ideologically superior. However by 1989 even among this group voluntarism was becoming a more acceptable option, and in Camden provision through the voluntary sector was already entrenched as a socialist initiative.

Policy developments

The 1980s was a decade when indoor sport provision began moving into a new phase. A changing political climate with an emphasis on the free market and the privatisation of public services saw local authorities re-examining and re-formulating their leisure policies. When such policies were first developed in the 1960s and 70s the emphasis had been on the building and provision of facilities. During the 1970s there was a shift in emphasis as patterns of use were established. Alongside continued building there was a growing belief that sports provision, like other social services, could play a role in improving the quality of life of the community and that this should be a primary objective of public sports providers. This second phase of sports policy was guided by social objectives with an emphasis on delivering opportunities to all sections of the population. During the 1980s this phase seemed to be closing as local authorities entered a period in which financial objectives were brought to the fore.

Impending compulsory competitive tendering (CCT), national government policies which restricted local authorities' spending, and the ideological approach of the Thatcher government were each contributing to this shift in emphasis in the six cities that we studied. The Audit Commission report *Sport for Whom?* (1989) argued for a new balance between financial and social objectives in public sport provision, and made it clear that in the Commission's judgement former policies had weighed too heavily on the social side of the equation. The need for cost-effectiveness to redress the balance was stressed. This report was highly critical of the practices of most local authority leisure departments, arguing that there had been a disregard for cost-effectiveness, a lack of any clear guiding strategy, quantifiable objectives and performance monitoring. One of the Audit Commission recommendations was that all public sport providers should have strategies which would be reviewed every five years. The strategies would include aims and objectives which could be quantified and monitored to check the effectiveness of provisions.

In the cities that we studied there were several common trends. Firstly, where strategies had existed in the past these had taken the form of broad guidelines but lacked specific objectives. The leisure departments had been guided by underlying philosophies rather than clear and quantifiable aims. Without these it was very difficult to implement effective monitoring to assess achievements. As they approached the 1990s the departments were recognising that existing strategies were out-dated, and were in the process of re-defining aims and objectives and producing new strategies in response to changing conditions. All the local authorities were in a period of flux in terms of philosophy and strategy. Old strategies were being replaced by new. Also, as the authorities were facing financial restrictions there was a shift in emphasis between social and financial considerations with the latter receiving growing attention. By the end of our research in 1989 the impending introduction of CCT was a major catalyst for the production of new strategies.

In 1986 Glasgow, Liverpool, Belfast, Cardiff and Camden (but not Chester) had been guided by recreation strategies of sorts. The emphasis was then on achieving satisfactory levels of provision throughout the cities, but the strategies also dealt with issues such as targeting and sport development. By 1989 these strategies were considered outdated. Building programmes either had been or were being completed to the extent that available capital would allow. Changing legislative and socio-economic conditions meant that new strategies were required.

The departments in all six cities were formulating strategies to deal with CCT. Progress in Chester had been exceptional. In 1986 any policy guidelines were scant. Yet by 1989 the main priority of the newly established leisure services department was the production of a guiding strategy. One feature of this was to be the creation of a corporate leisure organisation which would consider alternative sources of provision, particularly by encouraging private investment in sport. However, the main aims continued to be to increase participation and to provide a wide variety of quality services. Dual use was to continue to play an important part in provision; it was proving attractive because these centres would remain unaffected by CCT.

Cardiff was soon to fulfil a 10 year recreation building strategy and was considering different philosophies. The new aim was to offer access to sport for all the community *in a cost-effective manner*. Cost-effectiveness was already on the agenda in 1986 when managers were to provide an accessible service while generating the maximum compatible income. In 1989 Cardiff was moving towards a corporate approach and there were plans to produce a corporate document.

In Liverpool the 1983 strategy was proving inadequate in the face of new developments. There was a lack of clear aims and objectives, a phenomenon not unique to Liverpool. So by 1989 a new strategy was being produced to deal with CCT and changing leisure demands. The intention was to rationalise and improve existing provisions. Co-operation with the private sector was under consideration, although this was to be limited and subject to strict council control. Liverpool remained committed to a public leisure service accessible to all sectors of the community.

In 1986 Camden had an underlying philosophy that leisure services could make a crucial intervention analogous to those made by other social agencies in maintaining individuals' and communities' quality of life. Social objectives had played a primary role in directing policy. In 1986 breaking-even was not a priority for facility managers; reaching all sections of the community was placed above this. In contrast, by 1989 managers had been directed to become cost-effective, and there was a drive to reduce deficits. In 1987 the council had hit financial difficulties and staffing levels were cut. These difficulties, combined with CCT, had influenced departmental philosophy. Although the aims of 1986 still stood, by 1989 financial considerations were much higher up the agenda. Deficits had been reduced and prices were some of the highest in London. Camden still had service aims to which all managers were supposed to adhere as well as financial targets. The priorities had simply shifted, assimilating financial considerations. The new policy was to offer a broad range of leisure services for the greatest number of people as possible, but *within the constraints of money available.*

In Belfast in 1986 the department had the primary aim of providing and managing leisure facilities and offering a comprehensive programme of pursuits attractive to as many of the population as possible. As the department approached the 1990s and CCT, it felt that a reassessment and review of objectives was opportune. The social advantages of sport provision had previously been over-riding. Money had been readily available to act on proposals. By 1989, however, there had been a change in emphasis. Although the council had not abandoned social objectives, increasing weight was being placed on finance. Objectives were being reviewed, reflecting the need to become more cost conscious. In 1989, like other departments, Belfast was mid-stream between shedding an older philosophy and embracing a new creed. In 1988 Belfast had produced a new strategy document which had become policy. It enshrined a more commercial and flexible approach to leisure management. Potentially profit-making services were to be developed and joint projects with other sectors were to be considered. Facilities were to be upgraded to cater for changing leisure demands. It recommended, among other things, a corporate approach to leisure provision, a staff and pricing review, and greater management effectiveness. In two years Belfast had moved swiftly in these new directions. For example, pricing had been reviewed and increased. Another change had been the rationalisation of services. Staffing had been rationalised which had meant the loss of 112 posts involving 49 redundancies. At tier three centres opening hours had been reduced considerably and at the other centres opening was an hour later. The experience of Belfast was a clear example of the new directions in which public leisure provision was moving.

In Glasgow the 1985 recreation plan outlined policy until 1995. This recognised under-provision for indoor sport in the city and also the lack of capital to meet perceived deficiencies. It set out a development programme which consisted mainly of upgrading existing facilities combined with limited new building and the development of dual-use. It also set out policies dealing with targeting, management, marketing and sponsorship, stressed the need to maximise income, to attract new users by improved marketing, and envisaged a pricing structure which would reduce subsidies. Joint ventures with commercial organisations were proposed as one option in developing new sport opportunities during a period of limited public finance. However, Glasgow remained committed to providing a leisure service which would improve the quality of life for all residents, and aimed to increase sport participation. By 1990 a struggle to resolve financial and social objectives was taking place.

In trying to balance pressures of social and financial objectives, all the local authority departments were hoping that these would not prove mutually exclusive. Both were being incorporated into new strategies. Indoor sport facilities were to be provided in a cost-effective manner while remaining subsidised and providing a wide range of opportunities for all sections of the community.

Targeting

Despite financial pressures there were was still a commitment in every city to providing reasonably priced leisure services for residents. In each city the subsidy per user varied greatly between centres. There was also variation between activities and sessions, some generating much more income than others. Takings from these were often used to subsidise heavy loss-making sessions. The Audit Commission report (1989) was critical of blanket subsidies arguing that these usually meant working class ratepayers subsidising middle class users. Yet in cities such as Cardiff universal blanket subsidy was preferred to selective concessionary rates for disadvantaged groups. A passport scheme was available only for the disabled. Other groups paid a cheap standard rate or attended special sessions at which managers were able to offer a 50 percent discount.

In the other cities during the 1980s an element of selectivity had been introduced into pricing structures as an integral part of targeting. Certain groups were entitled to reduced charges or could obtain a "pass" which allowed reductions. Most local authorities had concessions for the unemployed (Glyptis and Pack, 1988). In 1986 Camden operated a leisure pass scheme which was unique in our survey areas, not because it offered free-use of facilities to the unemployed, disabled, OAPs and those receiving supplementary benefit, but because it offered free use with no restrictions on time. By 1989, however, this had been modified; free use was no longer unrestricted. The leisure pass had been replaced by a leisure card which for £5 a year gave use of facilities at a third of the normal cost. Those eligible were

OAPs, people with disabilities, the unemployed, students, trainee nurses, those in receipt of housing benefit, family credit or income support, and those on Employment Training. Other residents could purchase a card and were then entitled to a smaller reduction. From 1984 Liverpool had run a city-wide "Freesport" initiative. This entitled UB40 holders to free use of facilities at off-peak times. In Liverpool during our research this scheme was not restricted but extended to include other low income groups including dependents of the unemployed, individuals receiving any social security benefit, OAPs, and the registered disabled. Liverpool was the only city in our research that was still running a "Freesport" policy in 1989. Glasgow was continuing to operate a "passport to recreation" campaign which, for the cost of £1, offered use of all facilities at one third of the normal charge to the disabled, the unemployed, their dependents, and others on low incomes.

These price concessions were sometimes part of broader targeting strategies. In its policy documents and under the banner "Sport For All", the Sports Council (1982, 1988) had made it clear that reducing inequalities of opportunity should be a central aim of public sport providers. It had introduced the concept of target groups, identifying sections of the population whose participation rates lagged behind the general level. The Sports Council had highlighted the lower socio-economic groups, women, the disabled, ethnic minorities, the unemployed and the elderly for targeting. In its most recent policy documents it had also prioritised the 13-24 age group in recognition of the impact of sport experience in this life-phase on later participation, and due to the high drop-out rates in this age-group. The concepts and ideas involved in targeting had begun to be incorporated in many public providers' development strategies.

The degree of targeting in operation during our research varied from city to city. At one extreme a department would have a clear targeting policy; a co-ordinated programme of initiatives designed to attract selected groups. At the other extreme there would be a broad commitment to reach all sections of the community, then ad hoc provisions for a range of groups. The latter was the case in Chester which offered some women-only sessions and creches, and UB40 football. In Belfast and Cardiff the emphasis had been on blanket provision rather than selective targeting, and in 1989 these cities still had no clear policies on target groups. In Belfast any targeting was arranged by individual centre managers. In Cardiff some sessions for target groups had been provided by MSC-funded "Actionsport" teams. With the end of the Community Programme in 1988 many of these schemes had folded. Cardiff and Liverpool had tried to incorporate sessions previously run under "Actionsport" into their mainstream provisions. In Northern Ireland, however, "Operation Sport" teams were still organising sessions in public centres for women, the unemployed, and people with disabilities. In Liverpool there had never been a clear policy on target groups; there was simply a broad commitment to serving disadvantaged sections of the community. In 1986 Liverpool had a programme for encouraging use by the unemployed and a policy dealing with women. Otherwise management was simply guided by the broad aim of increasing participation. As in the other cities there were no clear guidelines. Such targeting as existed was ad hoc. Individual centres operated creches during certain hours. Pool lifts for the disabled, UB40 sessions, and women's sessions were available at some centres but not at others.

However, by 1989 there were signs of change. Liverpool's design and development section was producing a detailed targeting policy in which groups would be prioritised. The two groups that had received most attention in practice were women and the unemployed. Liverpool had gone further than any other city that we studied towards formulating a structured pro-gramme for women. In 1986 the council had launched a "Women in Sport" campaign which ran for several years. In 1987 a policy document "Building Bridges" was produced by a Women and Sport Working Party which made recommendations on how to encourage women and girls to participate. This was accepted as departmental policy, and subsequently the council employed a Women's Sports Development Officer to co-ordinate provisions. The outcomes were an extensive programme of women-only activities at *all* centres, increased training for women staff, and an effort to change the image of sports centres which had appeared to promote male sports. Indeed, in each city activities popular with women such as aerobics and keep-fit, as well as more traditional sports such as netball, were being given more centre space and programme time.

Glasgow had also selected women as a target group. In 1989 a co-ordin-ated programme was still being developed, though the city's sports centres already offered a wide range of women's activities. Belfast, Cardiff and Chester had not formally adopted women as a target group, but still provided a variety of sessions for women-only including weights, keep-fit, pre and post-natal swimming, and women's mornings sometimes with creche facilities. Many of these sessions were heavily subsidised and only low rates were charged.

Camden and Glasgow were the most advanced cities in terms of formulat-ing and operating targets. In 1986 Camden had already produced a targeting strategy. In the strategy document seven target groups were identified, but by 1989 Camden had decided to concentrate on just three. These were priori-tised in the light of findings from a major user survey which was conducted in 1989 to assess who they were hitting and missing. Only one percent of users were disabled, so they were confirmed as a target group, as were ethnic minorities and the over-50's.

Camden and Glasgow were both in the process of formulating special programmes for ethnic minorities. They were seeking support and advice from appropriate community organisations to ensure that they reflected the needs of minority communities. Despite having relatively large minority populations, Cardiff and Liverpool were doing little to promote ethnic minority participation. However, in Liverpool they were described as a second tier target group, and in Cardiff they were beginning to receive some attention. An example of targeted provision in this category was swimming sessions for muslim women.

The disabled had received some attention in all the cities. Subsidised sessions for the disabled were offered at many centres. In 1989 Camden had launched a strong drive to increase use of facilities by the disabled. A disabled person plus a carer with one cheaply obtained leisure pass could use all the department's facilities free of charge. This was combined with special sessions for people with disabilities, free swimming and, at one centre, a club for people of all ages with disabilities. In Glasgow special grants were available for disabled groups wishing to form clubs. Giving the disabled access to buildings had became an issue in every area. In Belfast a PHAB (physically handicapped and able-bodied) group had been set-up at one centre, and an integrated summer scheme had run for several years which brought able-bodied and physically disabled children together.

Camden was examining other local authorities' campaigns in order to decide which approach to adopt for its third priority group, the over-50s. They already offered, in addition to other concessionary schemes, free swimming and subsidised 50-plus sessions. In 1989 Glasgow, Cardiff and Belfast were running city-wide 50-plus campaigns. Special well-publicised sessions were being offered in various centres under the 50-plus banner.

In its recreation plan Glasgow had defined the target groups to whom departmental resources should be directed. Three such groups were selected. Two of these groups were unusual in that they were geographically based in areas which were given priority status due to their highly assessed social need. The third group was an age group, 13-24 year olds. Although these groups were accorded the highest priority, Glasgow's plan stated that this should not mean the exclusion of programmes for other target groups. In practice a similar, though less formal arrangement had developed in each city. Certain groups had been prioritised and were receiving primary attention, but at the same time less prolific schemes and sessions were organised for others. In 1989 Glasgow's philosophy remained the same, but different groups were being prioritised. The council had a revised set of principal target groups, namely women, ethnic minorities, young people, and low income groups such as the unemployed and families or individuals receiving other DSS benefits.

Glasgow was the only city to have adopted young people as a priority group. The main initiative towards young people was an athletics scheme which aimed to attract 1,000 school children per week to Kelvin Hall and Crown Point. A gymnastics programme had also been developed to attract young girls on the city's peripheral estates. In all the other cities dual-use of school facilities was being encouraged. There was an awareness of the high drop-out from sport among school-leavers, and a recognition of the importance of encouraging this group to participate because of the long-term implications for sports participation, but outside Glasgow no co-ordinated city wide programmes had been developed.

Targeting was still embryonic in most places, and even where it had been initiated, evidence as to whether the objective of increasing participation was being achieved was usually non-existent. Accurate monitoring of the uptake on schemes was rare. However, there were some exceptions. For example, as a result of closely monitoring its programme for the disabled in 1989, Camden could provide evidence of a significant increase in use by this target group.

Although there was a broad consensus as to which groups should be targeted, there was disagreement about which should be prioritised. There was also no consensus on how to reach target groups once identified. Programmes varied between the cities. Priorities broadly in line with the target groups suggested by the Sports Council had been adopted, but from within this range there had been a tendency to select a smaller set of groups. The advantage of doing this was that efforts could be concentrated. The alternative was to spread resources thinly.

As with overall strategies, targeting policies tended to be unclear and were in need of re-assessment in the light of changing use patterns and socio-demographic trends. The need to clarify targeting policy was becoming more urgent with CCT on the horizon. The local authorities needed to build into specifications clear guidelines about what should be provided for various groups. Fears that CCT would mean the end of targeting may have been premature. If the local authorities themselves did not win in-house bids, precise specifications which assimilated targeting policy were intended to ensure that contractors continued to provide for the groups in question.

Convergence

Although there was some variation between the local authorities' philosophies and even greater diversity in the facilities they offered, at the end of the 1980s their policies and practices were converging because they were all facing the same basic problems. In the late-1980s local diversity was being over-ridden by two forces, financial pressures and the imminence of CCT, which seemed likely to create a qualitatively different type of public leisure service.

Central government financial policies intended to restrain local authority spending – clawbacks and capping, then the Community Charge or "poll-tax" – were making an impact on sport provision as on other public services. Each city had experienced financial cutbacks and was formulating policies within mounting financial constraints. Between 1986 and 1989, despite central government efforts to restrain local government spending, outlay on leisure services had continued to increase in each of the cities. Capital spending had continued as some of the authorities completed new build, upgrading or alteration programmes as in Liverpool, Cardiff, Camden and Glasgow. Cardiff was planning further capital investment to build its final district centre which would complete the city's leisure plan. Glasgow was in the middle of a continuing programme of extending and upgrading its facilities. Throughout the 1980s some of the cities had been able to sustain capital building programmes, but by 1989 new funds for future developments were extremely scarce. By then there were clear signs of central government policies beginning to bite. Belfast leisure services had undergone rationalisation. Camden had been forced to reduce subsidies and staffing levels after financial difficulties, and any new developments which involved an injection of capital had to be in co-operation with the private sector. Partnership with the private sector was also seen as the most realistic way forward in Chester. Liverpool still hoped to complete its planned expansion of facilities, but the release of capital funds in the near future was unlikely, so arrangements with the private sector were being considered. The overall trend was to shift from direct public provision towards co-operative ventures in which the local authority played the role of an enabler. If the local councils were to meet the sporting, social and cultural interests of their citizens within financial constraints, it seemed that joint ventures would play important parts. Although local authorities through the 1980s may have been able to resist central government attempts to control their spending, they were unable to manage their leisure services unaffected by central government policies. The authorities in our study were making policy compromises because they simply did not have, and could not envisage themselves obtaining resources to implement their preferred policies. Like other public services, leisure departments were working within restricted budgets.

The Compulsory Competitive Tendering (CCT) legislation was to come into effect in 1992, requiring local authorities to put the management of sports centres out to competitive tender if they had not done so already. The impending introduction of CCT was perhaps the most powerful force shaping sports provision when our fieldwork ended in 1989. In readiness for CCT, the local authorities were undergoing rapid re-organisation and in some cases rationalisation. The need to prepare tender specifications, to set up direct service organisations, contractor units, if internal bids were to be made, and other CCT related re-organisation were commanding much time and resources.

In 1989 each of the local authority departments was in flux. In preparation for CCT, if they had not done so already, they were developing strategies, quantifying aims and objectives, clarifying and formulating policies. Indeed, they were reviewing their entire provisions in an attempt to run services more efficiently. One fundamental change was the re-organisation of the leisure departments to create a client-contractor split in order to deal with the requirements of CCT. Glasgow, Camden and Cardiff had already undergone structural re-organisation into two sections. Officers had been seconded to work on the client side, preparing specifications, examining service delivery and recommending improvements. All these departments were to make in-house bids. In Cardiff tenders were to be invited for all centres as a group and it was doubted whether a private operator would emerge who could compete with the local authority. Camden was drafting specifications for the district's main public centre. They aimed to run a full year on these specifications, identifying and then correcting problems, with the intention of running for a further year on revised specifications, then bidding successfully. Liverpool was preparing to split on a contractor-client basis and was to make an in-house bid. Chester's preparations for CCT were just beginning. A differentiation between client and contractor had still not been made in 1989, nor had a decision been reached as to how CCT would be approached although this was high on the agenda for the newly-formed department. CCT was to come into force in Northern Ireland 18 months later than on the mainland, yet the Belfast department was already preparing for its introduction. A council decision had been taken to make in-house bids, and political backing had been obtained for a departmental rationalisation. Following this rationalisation, Belfast was ready to bring in management consultants to advise on how best to make the contractor-client split.

All the departments intending to make in-house bids believed that they would retain the services. If for some reason they failed, they were confident that well-prepared specifications would ensure that services would be provided by contractors in line with council policies. In general the local authorities were reacting positively to CCT. Most were committed to retaining services in-house and had embarked upon improving delivery and cost-effectiveness in readiness to compete with the private sector. CCT was being treated as an opportunity to examine services and identify shortcomings. We found the local authorities putting their own houses in order. Even officers who were strongly committed to social objectives in leisure provision were trying to make the most of legislation that they had not originally welcomed. They seemed to have accepted many criticisms of the Audit Commission, particularly that services should be more efficient. Although public indoor sports provision remained heavily subsidised, in preparing for CCT all the local authorities were attempting to make certain services profitable or at least less costly. Annual running costs of the departments' services had increased alongside provisions. If any further expansion was to occur, the departments realised that they had no choice but to operate in a more cost-effective manner and to consider options such as partnership with the private sector. Even so, they had not abandoned their commitment to public provision as the most equitable way of providing all citizens with opportunities for sport participation. They were keen to prove that skills and working practices assumed to be exclusive to the private sector were not so: CCT had given them the impetus and opportunity to improve services, and to re-think and plan effective policies and strategies to best serve their communities.

A "new look" for leisure?

Amidst this shake-up in provision and policy, it was possible to detect the development of a "new look" for public leisure. Throughout the UK public leisure departments were entering a phase in which they had to keep up with the latest leisure trends if they were to satisfy the demands of consumers and encourage new participants. As facilities aged, funding had to be found to keep them at an acceptable level of presentation and, where possible, to modify them to cater for changing demands. Changing trends in the leisure market were prompting a fresh look at the types of facilities provided. Hence since 1986 the development of leisure pools and health suites within public centres.

The local authorities were trying to cast-off the traditional image of public leisure provision as basic and old-fashioned, catering for only a narrow range of sports. They were keen to pioneer new, modern leisure opportunities. Creating this "new image" involved adopting new policies and practices, improved marketing and publicity, performance monitoring and, most importantly, the creation of a corporate identity. In 1989 all the local author-ities in our study stressed that they were creating or intended to become corporate bodies with strategies which defined aims and objectives, thus creating corporate "images".

As an integral part of the development of a corporate image for public leisure services, the marketing and publicity of leisure centres was receiving more attention. The Audit Commission report had argued that poor market-ing lay at the heart of many local authorities' problems. Many of the latter had accepted that in the past their marketing had been poor, so they were beginning to employ more sophisticated publicity. They recognised that much of their earlier publicity material had been poor quality. By 1989 a more co-ordinated approach to publicity had been adopted in all the cities. Mar-keting and publicity officers had been appointed in some places, and the production of publicity materials had been centralised. Attempts were being made to improve customer services in terms of facility quality and customer reception.

Belfast had refined its publicity and marketing to the greatest degree. A marketing consultant had been hired to construct a strategy which had been adopted by the department. This included the adoption of quantifiable corporate aims and a training package for all staff. Belfast had also used an advertising agency which, among other things, had produced a television advert and video-cassette publicising the city's leisure facilities.

The Glasgow department had taken part in a city-wide "Glasgow Smiles Better" campaign. It had also co-ordinated a "Glasgow Smiles Better for Sport" campaign which publicised the city's sports centres. As part of a general departmental re-organisation in Glasgow, two marketing officer posts had been created. By 1989 Cardiff also had a specialist publicity section. In Camden and Chester the entire marketing and publicity processes had just been given a structured format. In Liverpool there was still little marketing in 1989, but this was something to which the department was attending in its re-organisation and new strategy.

Market research and monitoring the use of facilities in order to assess the effectiveness of policies were growing phenomena, yet still embryonic. It had been difficult to carry-out any effective monitoring when there were no clear targets, aims or objectives, which had often been the case in the past. However, computerised data collection and information systems were increasingly present in the departments. By 1989 centre managers in Belfast were producing monthly throughput data which was fed into a central data base. Managements had targets to work to, and the information they provided indicated whether they had met these. The Audit Commission report had stated that monitoring was vital for the efficient functioning of leisure services. Yet monitoring was proving an expensive process, and lack of finance was restricting what the local authorities could achieve. Belfast had been the subject of a National Sports Council and Sports Council for Northern Ireland enquiry into the application of management information systems to sports provision. Management consultants had advised on the adoption of corporate aims and an information system. By 1989 Glasgow had established a computerised monitoring system and had produced the first report based on the findings. In most cities monitoring was limited, but the use of information technology was increasingly being explored in all departments. So by 1989 a new type of public leisure service seemed to be evolving, emulating some practices of the commercial world; corporate images, setting targets, professional publicity and marketing, and performance monitoring.

The late-1980s were turbulent times within local authority leisure departments, though on the streets outside things were more settled. The actual facilities - the bricks, mortar and plate glass were not in flux. Indeed, with less cash than formerly for new developments, "the heritage" was overshadowing current plans in determining what was actually available. The main changes in the local authorities' actual facilities in the late-1980s were basically an extension of earlier trends – opening still more buildings, and upgrading. Standard user charges were pushed upwards, centre staffing was "rationalised", and subsidies became more selective. Again, however, most of these changes amounted to developments rather than reversals of earlier targeting strategies.

The following chapters describe who was using and benefiting from the provisions in the six cities, and assess whether changes in use during our research were attributable to developments on the supply side. Our evidence shows that in the late-1980s neither local patterns nor levels of sport participation were thrust into greater flux than formerly. This was partly because most of the turbulence was contained within the providing organisations. Another reason was that, as the next chapter explains, most adults' sporting habits were proving resilient. Yet our evidence also shows that, in the longer-term, the structure and level of demand for sport facilities were responding to supply. And our evidence offers clear pointers to the most likely long-term implications of the "new look" that public leisure provision was acquiring in the late-1980s.

3

SPORT CAREERS

Polarisation

In the 1987 interviews respondents were asked for details about all the sports that they had played regularly during every year in their lives from age 10 onwards. Hedges (1986) had previously established that most members of the public have sufficient powers of recall to reconstruct their personal leisure histories, at least for relatively structured activities such as sport that are normally played at specified times and places. From the analysis it emerged that over 97 percent of panel members who had played one or more sports during every year in their lives from age 16 to 30 thereafter continued to play regularly at least until age 35. In contrast, among those who were not playing at age 30, just 21 percent took-up a sport regularly at any point during the next five years. This sharp contrast was not a result of our sample being composed mainly of current participants: surveys among representative samples of the public give virtually identical results (Roberts, Minten et al, 1990). By age 30 some individuals are established on continuous sport careers which by then are unlikely to be disrupted for many more years. Others have lapsed and are unlikely to return.

It is often said that human behaviour is difficult to predict – much moreso than the phenomena studied by natural scientists. Leisure behaviour is said to be particularly unpredictable since individuals can choose according to their whims. In the case of sport, however, most present-day British adults' behaviour is highly predictable from their own past conduct. A minority play sport regularly throughout their adult lives. As explained below, most of these loyal players are active in several games throughout their sport careers and play more than once in a typical week.

These individuals reap most of the direct benefits from sport facilities that are supposed to serve the entire community. A larger number abandon sport when young and never return on a regular basis. In terms of sport participation, there is a clear polarisation between a loyal and highly active minority, and the inactive majority of adults. Of course, it is not the case that everyone who remains in sport into adulthood persists until death eventually intervenes. Drop-out occurs in all age-groups. This is one reason why the proportion of the population taking part in sport declines progressively, at least until middle-age according to our evidence (see chapter six). However, the heaviest drop-out is in youth and young adulthood. Approximately a fifth of all the sports played regularly by our sample between ages 16 and 19 were abandoned in any given year.

Thereafter the sport give-up rate declined swiftly to around a quarter of its late-teenage level. Young people are the age group with the highest sport participation rate but they are also the most likely to lapse. If teenage drop-out rates persisted for many more years the number of sport players aged over 25 would be miniscule.

There is some scope for increasing adult sport participation by reducing drop-out among established players in their thirties and forties. Three percent of our respondents who had played continuously from age 16 to 30 dropped-out before age 35. However, it is clear that adult participation would rise much more substantially if more young people were persuaded to remain loyal. They have the highest drop-out rate into which to make inroads, and, if more young people were retained, adult participation would rise considerably given the increased survival rates of sport careers once individuals are into their twenties.

Some respondents in our enquiry who lapsed when young had returned to sport later-on. As explained above, just over a fifth of the members of our panel who were not playing at age 30 resumed their sport careers sometime during the next five years. We have examples from every city of well-publicised sessions aimed, for example, at the over-50s or mothers with young children, restarting the formerly inactive. It appeared possible for any reasonably skilled sport promoter to restart dozens of "couch potatoes" per month, but retaining them in sport year after year was usually proving a rather different and more difficult proposition (see Bailey and Biddle, 1988; Robinson and Mutrie, 1988). When new sports centres had opened near to their homes, formerly inactive respondents had often visited, sometimes just to look around, but often to sample the facilities by swimming or participating in some other activity. Another year on, however, the regular adult users of new centres were mostly people who formerly played regularly elsewhere. Some of our respondents had moved repeatedly into and out of sport participation. According to our evidence, around a quarter of currently active adult participants have interrupted careers in sport. Individuals who lapsed from sport had not necessarily been lost for ever. Even so, the fact remained that there were far better chances of retaining individuals who had maintained unbroken sport careers since childhood than restarting others.

Sport is no different from the arts, and indeed, most other leisure activities in this respect (Hantrais and Kamphorst, 1987). The greater number of most people's lifetime leisure activities are initially practised by the individuals during childhood and youth. Most of us spend the rest of our lives using "leisure capital" acquired when young. There are massive continuities in leisure interests and behaviour from youth until retirement (see Scott and Willits, 1989). Teenagers typically dabble and experiment with a wide range of leisure interests, many of which are soon dropped. Thereafter people's leisure styles tend to become focused around a smaller number of retained pastimes. It is not just sport but many other types of out-of-home recreation that lose most of their regular participants during young adulthood.

Needless to say, one activity's losses can be another's gains. Although sports providers may divide the population into the active and inactive, most of the individuals who had lapsed from sport, usually when young, had not become bored and completely idle; they had simply preferred to make other uses of their time and money. There is intense competition for the public's leisure time and spending. We will return to this point later, but it is important to realise from the outset that individuals are likely to remain in sport only if their experience of this kind of leisure gives better value for their time and money than the alternatives.

Bound-in or locked-out

If individuals had retained sport or any other leisure interests within their adult lifestyles, they had tended to become locked-in. Our evidence suggests that in the case of sport this was neither mainly because they had "burnt their boats" by relinquishing other pastimes nor by pure habit. We will explain later that very few of our sample's long-term sport careers had been composed of exactly the same routines, year-in and year-out. Individuals had become locked-in by their desire to repeat satisfying experiences derived from physical recreation in the past. They also became bound into social networks in which sport activity was normal if not expected. Social pressure and the desire to maintain friendships had kept some participants in teams and clubs. Participation even in an individualistic sport such as sailing can supply the sense of belong to a real community that so many people find scarce in present-day society (Levy, 1989). It was also the case (as explained later in chapter eleven) that regular sport participants were exposed to, and were liable to absorb health and fitness values which then strengthened their motivation to remain active. The points to note here are, firstly, that all these attractions were growing in strength the longer sport careers ran, and secondly that the processes that bound-in some individuals were simultaneously locking-out others.

A common answer, given by 34 percent, when non-participants were asked what might persuade them to play sport, was simply "nothing". Nearly everyone (65 percent of all non-participants) who said that something might persuade them to resume sport mentioned "time". The next most common answer (by 43 percent) was "someone to participate or to go with". This illustrates how the non-participants were typically excluded by belonging to the wrong social networks from the point of view of facilitating sport activity, and by their time being otherwise committed. Far fewer non-participants mentioned lower charges (16 percent) or higher incomes (18 percent) as being likely to draw them back into sport. Similar, and relatively small proportions mentioned changed domestic circumstances (12 percent) or being relieved of the care of dependents, usually children (19 percent). Lacking the necessary time and the right social contacts were named as obstacles by larger numbers and, as explained later, participants experienced the pressure on their time as the major problem in remaining in sport.

When non-participants who said that "nothing" would persuade them to resume were invited to elaborate, 45 percent said that they were just "not interested", 31 percent described themselves as "too lazy", while 28 percent mentioned family responsibilities. Most of these individuals obviously saw themselves as non-sporting people who had other, more pressing commitments. Relatively few referred to health problems (13 percent) or to not being good at sport (15 percent). Most of those who said that absolutely "nothing" would persuade them to participate were probably telling the blunt truth. Adults who abandoned sport years ago could have difficulty imagining themselves as serious competitors in sports halls. Some could have been embarrassed by their physical condition, and others by their lack of sports competence. Young people may be prepared to take risks and "make fools" of themselves, but adults tend to feel under a greater obligation to "act their age". Most 30 and 40 year olds who had remained in sport were competent performers. Novices of their age were likely to stand out like sore thumbs. Adult non-participants also faced the need to break through the barriers erected by the social networks that locked-in established players. Furthermore, most non-participants had alternative leisure interests and social commitments. Why should they risk their time and money on sport when they had other things to do from which they could rely on social, psychic or physical rewards?

Social research is often accused of merely discovering what everyone else already knew. We anticipate such reactions to our advocacy of reducing drop-out during young adulthood as the best strategy for boosting participation in later life. In fact, however, great efforts have been made to reclaim lapsed adults. There were examples in every city that we studied. In contrast, young people were a primary target group in only one of the cities (Glasgow). An alternative common-sense view had been that young people were the age group with the highest participation, so why give them more encouragement? Sports management in the UK has not normally been sensitive to the fact that young people have the heaviest rate of retirements.

Comparisons of the sport biographies of different age groups in our own and other research suggest that overall participation rates in Britain have risen since the 1960s mainly as a result of more young adults being retained in sport, then carrying this activity into later life-phases (Boothby et al, 1981; Roberts et al, 1989). We suspect that very little of the rise in participation over the last generation will have been due to formerly inactive 30, 40, and 50 year olds being persuaded to resume, then remaining sports active. Rather it appears that more 16-25 year olds have been retained in sport, and have then carried their higher propensity to participate into their 30s, 40s and 50s.

This implies that seeking quick returns will be unrealistic and probably counter-productive in a sustained drive towards sport for all. The extremely low level of sport activity among the present-day over-50s is largely a product of their extremely high drop-out rates when they were teenagers many years ago. Special sessions, backed by imaginative marketing, had produced immediate surges in participation among over-50 year olds in some centres that we studied, but most of these resumptions were proving temporary. The eventual increase in later-life sport activity was likely to be larger and more solid if it arose from further reductions in drop-out among teenagers.

Early sport socialisation

Finding the right answers usually depends on asking appropriate questions. Explaining why some, but not all adults play sport is not a matter of discovering why some take-up physically active recreation in their 20s, 30s or 40s while others fail to do so. Most adult participants simply continue a kind of leisure behaviour which they have enjoyed since childhood. It is non-participants who change at some point in their lives by dropping-out.

Virtually everyone is involved in physically active recreation when young. If informal games in streets and parks are counted, sport participation is near universal among children and young people of both sexes (McCusker, 1985). So why do some drop-out shortly afterwards while others persist? We spent much time and effort inspecting our data but failing to find clear answers because initially we were looking in the wrong places. We were trying to discover what happened as individuals moved into adulthood that resulted in some breaking from sport while others continued. Would the answer lie in the transition from education, into married life, parenthood, moving house or becoming established in an occupational career thereby losing one's former companions, facilities or leisure time? Actually the main answer as to why some sport careers became long-running while others were disrupted lay earlier in the individuals' lives, in their experiences in sport during childhood and youth. Our evidence shows that provided young people had been given secure foundations in sport, the chances were that they would continue into adulthood whatever happened in other life domains. The members of our panel who became sufficiently committed when young seemed to have found ways of continuing in sport whatever their subsequent employment and domestic circumstances.

What did laying secure foundations mean? It could not be just a question of playing sport when young because virtually everyone had done this. Nor could it be a matter of simply enjoying or being particularly good at sport. Most children enjoy games, and there are thousands of inactive adults who can recall being quite good at particular sports when at school. Nor, according to our evidence, had the sheer quantity of sport played when young made the crucial difference. Rather, the characteristic that distinguished the early sport socialisation of the adults in our panel who persisted was the *number of different sports* that they had played regularly and in which they became proficient during childhood and youth.

Among the adults in our panel with unbroken careers, 64 percent had played three or more sports regularly between ages 16 and 19. Among those with interrupted sport careers, meaning that they had played at some time since age 20 but not during every year since then, only 20 percent had played regularly in three or more sports when in their late teens. Needless to say, the individuals who had never played any sport since age 20 reported less exposure earlier-on than all other groups of respondents. Figure 3.1 traces the sport biographies from age 10 to 20 of three groups of the respondents who were aged over 20 at the time of the research: those who had played at least one sport regularly during every year to up to their present ages, those who had never played any sport regularly since age 16, and an intermediate group.

Figure 3.1

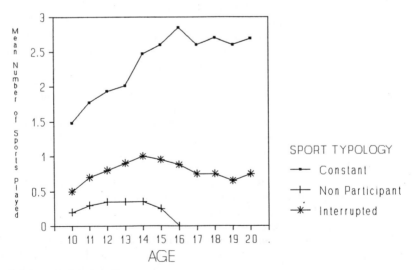

Mean Number of Sports Played
from age 10 to 20.
and Sport Career Typology

SPORT TYPOLOGY

●— Constant

+— Non Participant

＊— Interrupted

(Includes years not played)

At age 10 the individuals who were to build uninterrupted careers extending into adulthood were already playing the largest number of sports on average. Thereafter, up to age 15, they enlarged their ranges of sports more strongly than either of the other groups. By age 16 they were playing roughly three times as many sports on average compared with individuals whose post-16 participation was interrupted.

Most of the continuous players in our sample had always maintained several sports in their repertoires. At the time of our 1987 survey, 83 percent of over 20 year old respondents with uninterrupted sport careers were playing two or more sports regularly, and 27 percent were participating in four or more. Most of the participants were initially recruited to our study because they were taking part in one or another of the seven sports that were targeted in our facility surveys, but the eventual sample was not neatly divided into soccer players, swimmers and so on. Indoor bowls had the highest proportion of participants who were playing no other sport (56 percent). Bowls also had the oldest participants, and we explain in chapter five that a general trend with advancing age was towards playing fewer sports. Soccer had the lowest proportion of players, just five percent, who were involved in no other sport at the time of our 1987 survey. In each of the remaining sports that were originally targeted (martial arts, badminton, snooker, swimming, and keep fit/weight training) the proportions of singletons were between 12 and 17 percent. In every activity except bowls it was the exception, not the rule, for players to be involved in just the one sport. There was not even a natural division between participants in competitive and other sports. Rather, it was common, for example, for badminton players to swim regularly. Nor was there a clear division between participants in strenuous and non-energetic sports. Any clustering was due mainly to the same games tending to appeal to the same age and sex groups. For instance, snooker and soccer tended to be young men's games, and it was common for the same individuals to be involved in both.

Why should the number of games that people had played when young have been so influential over whether or not their sport careers extended into adulthood? Firstly, as explained later-on in chapter five, the sports that our respondents were most likely to play varied from stage to stage in the life-cycle. Team games that were popular among young people, and which were organisationally convenient when large numbers were gathered together for educational purposes, had proved far less convenient at subsequent stages in life. Games that could be played alone or by just two persons, who could participate at times of the day and week to suit their personal schedules, were more likely to be played into adulthood. This meant that dedication to a single team game such as soccer was unlikely to lay the foundations for life-long sport activity no matter how keenly and frequently a person had taken part as a teenager.

Secondly, the typical unbroken sport career in our sample had involved some reconstruction every two or three years when one sport had been dropped or another added. Very few participants with long-running sport careers had played exactly the same games persistently, year in and year out. This is why pure habit could not have been the main force that kept their sporting lives going. Sport give-ups had been quite frequent events even in uninterrupted careers in which the individuals had never dropped-out of all sport. Thirty-nine percent of the respondents in the final phase of our research in 1988 had given-up at least one sport during the previous two years, though only nine percent of those who were first contacted in the 1986 facility surveys had ceased playing sport altogether by the end of our project. The point about wide repertoires was that, whatever their reasons for dropping-out of particular sports, when the individuals played several games their entire sport careers were less vulnerable. If at least one sport was kept going, the individuals remained in social networks which offered introductions to teams and clubs through which games that the subjects may have played earlier in their lives could be resumed.

Some reconstructions had been forced or prompted by changes in other areas of the individuals' lives, but we do not wish to exaggerate the strength of these relationships. In the sample's sport biographies since age 10 there was a slightly higher than normal give-up rate during years also marked by other life events such as leaving education, changing jobs, becoming unemployed, moving house, marrying or separating, but these relationships were weak and often non-existent within particular age and sex groups (see Roberts, Minten et al, 1990). In the 1988 interviews we gathered detailed information about changes in the subjects' lives during the previous two years - whether they had changed jobs, moved into or out of the labour market, had a partner who had experienced either of these changes, moved residence, changed marital status, or experienced a change in income. The more of these events that individuals had experienced (with a drop being the crucial direction of change in income) the more likely was their sport participation to have declined between 1987 and 1988. However, even when the changes were combined into a single index of the extent to which individuals' lives had been disrupted, the relationship with changes in sport participation was not significant statistically.

We looked particularly closely at the effects of having experienced unemployment between 1986 and 1988. The group that had been unemployed throughout increased its sport activity marginally between 1987 and 1988, while the steepest decline was recorded by the group that moved out of unemployment. However, this relationship, like all the other connections between sport participation and wider life events, did not reach statistical significance. We are not disputing the accuracy of the findings from other research which show that the unemployed have particularly low rates of sport activity, but our evidence suggests that this is most likely to be due to groups whose sport participation is low to begin with having the greatest risks of unemployment. Within our sample, provided they were already involved in sport, individuals had typically continued to play throughout periods of unemployment. This evidence confirms that once individuals were established on careers in or out of sport, they were most likely to continue whatever happened in other life domains.

Movements out of and into different sports during continuous careers seemed to have their own momentum. Most sport career reconstructions appeared to have been at the players' own accord rather than prompted by life events. Players had often switched their games, teams and clubs upon losing interest in their former activities. Their main motivation appeared to have been to sustain novelty, unpredictability and excitement in their sporting lives. The psychic rewards from sport are known to diminish once one's own performance becomes predictable either relative to an objective measuring device such as a clock or to the opponents who compete in a particular club or league (see Chick and Roberts, 1989). Many sports institutionalise breaks by organising play into seasons, and sustain unpredictability by reconstructing leagues through promotion and relegation, and through informal "player markets" which encourage individuals to move to clubs where they will encounter matched opposition. Over and beyond this, however, the players in our sample had kept their sport interest and careers alive by switching games. And the more sports in which they were proficient, the more able were players to use this strategy.

Another advantage of breadth was in enabling the players to maintain balanced sporting lives. Many of our respondents had main sports that they played seriously, while others were practised more for fun, in a recreational spirit, or just to help to keep in condition. Professional players typically regard their main sport as "a job" for which they are paid, and do not necessarily expect to enjoy playing (Roadburgh, 1977). Amateurs have less reason than professionals to accept the routine and discipline involved in simply maintaining the highest standards of which they are capable in their best sports.

Attitudes

We asked a battery of questions on attitudes towards sport. Non-participants were asked what might persuade them to play, while participants were asked why they took part. Everyone was asked for their views on the features of a good sports centre, about the drawbacks and advantages of sport participation, and the kinds of people who were most likely to benefit. Respondents who increased or reduced their sport activity during the research were asked for their reasons, and likewise if they changed the centres at which they played indoor sports.

All these questions pointed towards the same conclusions as regards the sample's main motivations towards, satisfactions derived from sport, and the perceived costs. Sport was seen as enjoyable in itself and for the social contacts, with the additional advantages of keeping one fit and healthy, and feeling good. There were only minor differences between the views of men and women, in different age groups, from different social classes, and by levels of sport activity. According to our evidence, there is a broad consensus throughout the UK public on the main costs and benefits of playing sport. It was not their different attitudes that were keeping some apart from, and others in sport (see also Crombie et al, 1990; Rayner et al, 1990).

The main reasons given by participants for taking part in sport were enjoyment (80 percent), the health and fitness benefits (72 percent), the feeling of psychological well-being that resulted (57 percent), and the opportunities to meet and mix with other people (56 percent). More or less the same answers were given to our question to the entire sample about the advantages of taking part in sport: fitness (78 percent), health (74 percent), social contact (74 percent), and enjoyment (69 percent). When individuals increased their participation, their most frequent explanations were that they found sport enjoyable and to keep fit.

The most common answer to our question on who could benefit from sport was "everyone" (70 percent). When particular categories of people were named, these were usually the unfit and unhealthy (66 percent), those with sedentary jobs and lifestyles (60 percent), disadvantaged groups such as the lonely (57 percent) and the unemployed (52 percent), and young people and children (50 percent). Sport was not seen as being most beneficial for fit and active individuals, or those with exceptional talent.

When asked about the disadvantages of sport activity, 46 percent of all respondents could think of none. The drawbacks mentioned most often were the risk of injury and damage to health (52 percent), pressure on time (33 percent), the expense (30 percent), and having less time for one's friends and family (26 percent). When individuals reduced their participation their most common explanations were lack of time (37 percent), poor health (17 percent), and loss of interest (12 percent). Just under a third of the sample mentioned the financial costs as a disadvantage, but money was rarely given as a reason for individuals reducing their own participation, or by non-participants for not taking part. All groups were far more likely to mention time than money in explaining their own sport behaviour. When individuals changed their places of play, their most common explanation was ease of access (37 percent), followed by there being better facilities at the preferred centres (18 percent).

The demands of sport

Sport was proving a demanding leisure activity because deriving the main benefits (health, fitness, feeling good, and the social relationships) depended on taking part regularly and quite frequently. Respondents with uninterrupted sport careers were usually active in more than one game, and were playing several times per week altogether. Sport occupied a demanding position in these individuals' leisure time budgets. The financial costs were not negligible, but time was the main scarce commodity that had to be deflected from other possible uses.

In addition to time and money sport was demanding technical ability and social skills. Those who argued that virtually anyone could become sufficiently competent to enjoy sport were usually fairly skilled themselves. People had been unlikely to stay in sport throughout their adult lives unless they were sufficiently competent for participation to have positive effects on their self-regard. Maybe the non-participants were capable of gaining this level of competence, but if they had failed to do so when young they were unlikely to feel it worthwhile to risk the necessary time and effort later in life.

One of the advantages of playing sport was seen as the social contact, but the opposite side of this coin was that sport was making social demands. Individuals had to cope with joining teams and clubs, and finding and retaining partners with whom to play. These demands were continuous because most long-running sport careers involved repeated reconstruction. Those who possessed the necessary social skills experienced the social side of sport as a benefit, but to other people the social demands were a barrier. Once again, the best time for acquiring the relevant social relationships and skills had been during childhood and youth.

We questioned the sample about some items of their spending on sport – membership fees, admission and travel costs, and specialist journals. We did not ask about equipment or clothing partly because such items can be very occasional purchases and we suspected that respondents would find it difficult to judge exactly how much they spent per week or year, and also because footwear, shirts and shorts, for example, may not be purchased for particular sports, or even just for sport but as general leisure attire. This means that our figures for personal spending on sport are under-estimates. However, in 1987 the typical player in our sample was spending £3.20 per week on travel, admissions, membership fees and journals. This was not an enormous sum: it often amounted to less than £1 per hour of play, which made sport a fairly cheap form of out-of-home recreation. Even so, the cost could well have been sufficient to deter low income groups, including some young people. It is also the case that households' finances are often stretched during the family formation life-stage. According to our evidence, maintaining two adults' sport careers normally cost £6.40 per week in 1987, excluding equipment and clothing. When children's play had to be supported the total costs would have been even higher. Again, it is easy to understand why adults who had lost touch with sport lacked the motivation to commit themselves to these regular outlays.

Then there was the time problem. Fifty-six percent of the players in our sample were actually playing sport for at least four hours per week, not counting travelling, changing and socialising time. Fifteen percent were playing for more than 12 hours per week in total. Each individual was given a participation score with 10 points awarded for weekly participation in one sport, 70 for daily participation, and pro rata. In 1987 the participants' mean score was 47.7, representing just under five times per week. Of course, it was possible to play sport with less dedication than our typical respondent. Many players in our sample were participating more occasionally. But the frequent players were not the most likely to become burnt-out and withdraw. They were the participants who were the most likely to have continuous sport careers stretching back to childhood.

The demands, especially the time demands of sport participation for our sample were often heavy. Deriving the full benefits seemed to depend on individuals allowing sport to consume so much time as to have inevitable implications for other household members. Perhaps this makes it easier to understand why sport had either become a lifelong leisure activity from youth onwards, or else adults were likely to remain apart permanently. Unless lifestyles incorporating sport had been adopted and maintained in young adulthood, individuals were unlikely to have reshaped their entire leisure habits to accommodate regular participation. They had built-up other interests and commitments, and could not be sure from personal experience that the effort of breaking into sport would prove worthwhile for them.

Policy implications

If it was just a matter of persuading young people to participate in several games instead of "doing nothing" the task of sport promotion would be relatively easy. The reality, however, is that there is intense competition for everyone's leisure time and money, and as we have shown, sport makes heavy demands, especially on time. The evidence in later chapters shows that whether the young people in our sample were acquiring the breadth of sports interests and skills that were likely to sustain long-term careers was sensitive to their ease of access to low cost facilities.

From the point of view of promoting lifelong sport for all, our evidence suggests that recent trends in sport education and provision in the UK have been in the right directions. The best way to maximise long-term participation will not be to encourage teenagers to concentrate on the particular sports in which they excel. Nor will it be sensible for schools or youth organisations to concentrate on producing winning teams in a limited range of sports. The governing bodies of what have hitherto been the UK's major sports – rugby, soccer and cricket for example – have expressed alarm that fewer young people are achieving high standards in these particular games. These concerns are probably justified, but the trend among young people has not been out of sport but towards spreading their interests across a wider range of activities, and our evidence suggests that the eventual effects in terms of adult sport participation will be positive.

The advantages of broad sporting repertoires endorse the policy of catering for sport in multi-purpose facilities rather than in single-sport clubs. And the enhanced survival rates of sport careers that begin with broad bases indicate why facilities are so important. In principle it is possible to become a sport participant without any special facilities or equipment. All one needs is suitable footwear in which to run or jog. Exercising at home need not require even this. In practice, however, our evidence shows that long-term sport careers had rarely been based upon individuals becoming dedicated runners or home exercisers when young then persisting with these particular activities ever after. The broad-based repertoires on which long-term sport careers had usually drawn had demanded special facilities and equipment, and someone had to provide these resources.

4

SPORT, GENDER AND SOCIAL CLASS

Sex differences

It is well-known that more men than women play sport, but our evidence shows that this does not apply in every sport or every sports centre. Among the areas where our research was based there was one local authority, Camden, where as many women as men were using the public sector facilities in 1989. It is interesting that this seemed to have happened more through the force of local demand than by particularly strenuous targeting, and a single case is proof that although up to now male dominance in sport has been normal, this is not an inevitable fact of life to which everyone has no alternative but to adjust. Needless to say, in 1989, when sex parity had been achieved in Camden's public facilities, it was impossible to say whether this example of equal opportunities would prove long-standing.

In 1986, at the time of our facility surveys and in the sports on which we focused, male users outnumbered women overall in every age group from youth to old age. Moreover, our following surveys found that the women participants were playing fewer sports than the men, for less time per week in total, were spending less overall and per session, and were the more likely to abandon sport completely during the course of our research. Males who were not taking part in any sport when first contacted were more likely than women non-players to return to sport prior to the conclusion of our field-work in 1988. On every single measurement that we made, women's attachments to sport, where applicable, were the more precarious, while in other cases their exclusion was the more rigid. However, there was considerable variation in the extent to which sport was male dominated depending partly on the policies and priorities of the local authorities and centre managements.

Gender and early sport socialisation

Children were outside our research brief, but there was evidence that, in their childhoods, our male respondents had been given the greater encouragement to play sport by parents and teachers. By age 10, when our records of respondents' sport biographies commenced, the boys were generally playing more sports than the girls (see also chapter six) and from that point onwards male dominance in sport was lifelong. The boys and girls may have had nominally equal opportunities for physical recreation in their schools, but it is known that teenage girls have resorted to numerous strategies to avoid school games (Scraton, 1987). Many have dropped-out of sport for ever at the earliest opportunity, namely, on becoming eligible to leave full-time education. Our subjects' sport biographies show that in general the males had played more sport as teenagers. There was a higher drop-out rate from sports in young adulthood than at any other life-stage among both sexes, but we know that up to now this early flight from sport has been strongest among females who have been the least involved sex to begin with.

The pressures that have pushed young women out of sport are well-known. Boys have found sport useful in establishing masculine identities. Indeed, they have typically been encouraged to play and excel in sport: the required qualities of strength and competitiveness have been admired in members of their sex. Teenage girls have been more likely to find sport a hindrance in establishing their feminity. Modern sports were developed initially by and for men who never intended to encourage girls to nurture their strength and to sweat to exhaustion in a desire to win (Lensky, 1988). However, there is recent evidence of female teenagers differing from males not in being less likely to regard sport as suitable for their sex, but only in the particular sports judged appropriate (Archer and McDonald, 1990). Up to now young females have been further disadvantaged in access to sport by the prevalent expectation that finding then supporting a male will be their principal leisure interest (Griffin, 1985). Teenage boys have been the more encouraged and motivated to preserve their own peer groups and leisure activities. Needless to say, this pattern has tended to continue throughout the life-cycle: males have claimed a right to leisure on the assumption their schedules should take precedence (Hantrais, 1985), and that women will take care of their domestic maintenance, while women's pleasures have often been derived from or between servicing the play of other family members (Deem, 1982, 1986; Green et al, 1987, 1990; Wimbush and Talbot, 1988). Sport has possibly been the prime example of men's leisure being claimed as a right, often at the expense of women's (Barrett et al, 1989; Dempsey, 1990; Thompson, 1990). Our evidence does not dispute that up to now these have been among the social facts of life, but it shows that females' disadvantages in access to sport can be remedied by appropriate provisions.

Gender and attachment to sport in adulthood

Given the impediments that previous cohorts of young women must somehow have circumvented to remain in sport, we half-expected that the exceptional minority of female adults who had survived would be as committed to, and as persistent in sport as adult male players. In fact this was not generally the case (see also Dench, 1988). The males in our panel were playing more sports on average, for more time per week. As explained in chapter three, the total amount of time that each respondent in our survey was devoting to sport was calculated by awarding 10 points for weekly participation in any game, 70 points for daily participation and pro rata. In the 1987 survey male and female participants averaged 56 and 41 points respectively, and 53 and 38 in 1988. In 1987 40 percent of the male participants in our panel were playing for more than eight hours per week in total compared with just 18 percent of the female players. Twenty-six percent of the male players were taking part regularly in four or more sports in 1987 compared with just 15 percent of the women participants. The women who were playing in 1986 were slightly more likely than the men to reduce or withdraw from participation by 1987 (35 and 30 percent), while a slightly higher proportion of the male players in 1986 had increased their sport activity by 1987 (18 and 15 percent). The women who were playing in 1987 were more likely than men to reduce or withdraw by 1988 (45 and 40 percent), and once again more men increased their participation (38 and 33 percent). Among all the respondents who had played any sport regularly since age 20, 63 percent of the men but only 48 percent of the women had kept-up at least one sport during every year.

Some of the above percentage differences are small, but the crucial point is that however the sample's involvement in sport was measured, the male players always appeared the more committed and involved. The male participants were spending more on their sport – an average of £4.02 per week compared with £2.50 by the women in 1987. This was not only because the men were playing more frequently; they were also spending more per sport session. For example, men who played once or twice a week were spending an average of £2.37 compared with £1.38 by females with identical participation rates. Males who played five to seven times per week in total were spending an average of £5.09 compared with £3.96 by equally active women.

Sex and attitudes to sport

However, on all our attitude questions there were only minor differences between males' and females' responses. They saw much the same advantages in, and reported the same benefits from sport participation – intrinsic enjoyment, sociability, and gains in health and fitness. They also recognised the same disadvantages – the risk of injury, and having less time to do other things. Both sexes were far more likely to mention the time than the money costs of sport participation. Overall, the females were just as likely as the males to mention advantages, and were no more likely to list disadvantages. When they had increased or reduced their sports activity, the sexes' reasons were similar, and likewise when they had changed the centres where they played. Lack of time and worsening health and fitness were both sexes' most common reasons for withdrawing or playing less. The availability of particularly good and nearby facilities, and friends who supplied introductions and encouragement, had been the main enticements when men and women had changed the centres where they played.

There was also very little difference in the sexes' behaviour prior to and after playing their sports (see Dench, 1988). They travelled to sports centres using similar transport, usually private cars, either alone or with the people they would play with. Afterwards there was little difference in the sexes' likelihood of socialising at or away from the sports centres. Thirty percent of the males and 32 percent of the female players in our 1986 facility surveys did so: the majority of both the men and the women went straight home after their games.

The males and females tended to play different sports, and the former were the more heavily involved, but in other respects the men and women were not participating in sport in specifically masculine and feminine ways, or for sex-specific reasons. The sexes' motives for taking part in sport and their criteria when evaluating centres were virtually identical. Both sexes regarded the main points about a good centre as being clean, friendly and convenient. Very few women regarded creche facilities as important. Indeed, this received the lowest rating of all the 15 characteristics that the sample was asked to rank. Our evidence suggests that making child-care available at all the sports centres would have made little impact on women's overall levels of participation. There were three main reasons for this. Firstly, the majority of women in our survey areas were withdrawing from sport before they became mothers. Secondly, most women today are in charge of young children for very few years during their adult lives. Thirdly, and perhaps most importantly, one of the aspects of their sporting lives that the women participants obviously valued was that they could be with their own friends, pursuing their own interests, which usually meant away from their families.

The similarities outweighed the contrasts, but there were still some interesting sex differences in the sample's attitudes. Firstly, the men were the more competitive. They were the more likely to explain their participation in terms of enjoying competition (35 against 15 percent), and improving their skills or performances (37 against 23 percent). These features of sport were also named by more males when respondents were asked to list the advantages of participation. When they had recently increased their sport activity, more men than women explained this in terms of wanting to improve their standards of play (14 against 6 percent). Also, when they had changed centres, men were the more likely to have been attracted by better equipment or clubs (22 against 13 percent).

Secondly, time was prominent in both sexes' answers to the above questions but with a subtle difference in emphasis. Men were more likely than women to explain why they were playing less (41 against 33 percent) and, if not participating at all, the circumstances that might persuade them to do so, in terms of simply lacking or needing more time. Women's answers to these questions placed more emphasis on access and nearness to facilities. Thirty-one percent of female non-participants compared with 18 percent of the males gave nearer facilities as a condition for taking part in sport. Also, women were more likely to mention convenience and travel problems when they had changed their centres (22 against 13 percent).

There were other feminine emphases. Women were more likely to mention lacking someone to go with as a reason for non-participation (50 against 31 percent), and were the more likely to see sport as especially beneficial for lonely (56 against 48 percent) and unemployed people (63 against 50 percent). Also, women were the more likely to mention "losing weight" as a reason for participating (33 against 15 percent), and keeping fit (22 against 15 percent) as a reason when they had increased their sport activity. Interestingly, few women mentioned domestic responsibilities as a reason for not playing sport or for playing less. This is unlikely to have been because these women's leisure was not handicapped by their domestic commitments. Those who listed "time" problems were often referring to their time being committed at home. However, the women participants seemed to have negotiated solutions to their domestic obligations, while the non-participants had other principal reasons for remaining outside sport.

The drawbacks of being a woman

It did not appear to be women's own attitudes to sport that were keeping some out, driving-out some who were playing, and otherwise preventing them participating as much as men, so much as the general leisure disadvantages of being female in present-day society. These include females having less time of their own, and being less able than men to claim leisure at times of their own choosing (Green et al, 1990). Women also have lower earned incomes on average, and spend less on their own pleasures than men. This means that even when women survive the social and cultural obstacles constructed by the masculinity of sport, the broader division of labour by gender continues to pull them back. The special impediments to women's participation are not all created by sport and its providers, but our evidence shows that this does not mean that providers can do little or nothing towards creating equal opportunities.

Catering for women

More men play sport than women overall, but the sex balance varies considerably from sport to sport. In the soccer and snooker sessions that we covered in the facility surveys, less than two percent of all players were female. Women's soccer was being offered at some centres but without any real success. Some snooker clubs were giving table time to promising young females, but otherwise virtually all the women around the tables were the companions of male players. Women were better represented in martial arts (24 percent), bowls (37 percent), swimming (40 percent) and badminton (47 percent). Weights rooms were generally male dominated, but most exercise classes were women's sessions, so overall 56 percent of the participants were women in these combined activities. Most centres were offering some sports that appealed to women, and the majority had some women-only sessions. However, there was considerable variation in the amounts of time, especially the amounts of prime time, that women's groups and sports were being given. Tokenism may have its uses, but a sprinkling of women's sessions was always likely to draw female players into marginal enclaves, sometimes from other sessions and centres.

Ultimately it is probably a question of power. It is still the case that more adult males than females are active in sport which means that neutral management of facilities will generally lead to male dominance. However, there are sufficient marginal players (see chapter five) – males and females whose participation or non-participation hinges on opportunity – for the management of sport facilities to make a difference, given the will. Up to now sport has been an arena in which men have been able to assert and display masculine superiority with women on the sidelines. This has been among the obstacles to women's participation. But this same fact makes sport a resource that women can use to assert and demonstrate their independence, thereby challenging the beliefs on which patriarchy rests.

In general the centre managements that we studied were finding it easiest to fill sports halls by allowing local soccer leagues to take over. Established users were liable to complain if women's groups with smaller memberships and no competitive track records were given precedence. Maybe Camden was in a favourable situation with large numbers of young women who worked and lived in central London on whom to draw, while the local males could find other London facilities for their games. In other areas it could prove far more difficult to draw women in. The fact that women spend less per session than men will reduce their attractiveness to centre managements who are under pressure to balance their books or reduce deficits. Camden still proves that women's under-representation in sport is not intractable but can be changed.

Class, cash and sport

Class or socio-economic status is related to sport in numerous ways. Particular sports tend to draw players from particular classes. Unsurprisingly, the prosperous are well-represented in sports such as polo and ocean racing where the equipment and facilities are expensive. However, the relationships between class, money and sport participation are not always so straightforward.

The working class participants in our sample were generally spending less on sport than middle class players. The latter were spending £3.60 a week on average compared with the former's £2.80. Some sports involved much heavier outlays than others. Among the seven sports from which our participants were originally drawn, martial arts was proving the most costly. Players were spending an average of £3.20 per week on admissions, membership fees and journals for this sport alone. It was followed, at some distance, by snooker (£1.98), then keep fit/weights (£1.57) and badminton (£1.51). The cheapest sports were swimming (£0.96), bowls (£1.03) and soccer (£1.16). At the centres where we conducted our user surveys the proportions of working class players did not rise smoothly from the most expensive to the cheapest sports. The sport with the highest proportion of working class participants was among the cheapest, bowls, but the sports with the next highest proportions of working class players were the most expensive – martial arts and snooker.

Needless to say, social class is not just a matter of money. It is related to how much participants can afford to spend, but our evidence shows that it was also related to who individuals chose to play with, the clubs they belonged to, and the centres that they used. This is not to say that the players were necessarily class conscious, or that those from the higher social strata were deliberately using sport to signal their class positions and wished to exclude the "lower orders". It was rather just a matter of how affairs were inevitably tending to work-out in an unequal society. People tend to work and play among, and marry their social equals. Since sport is part of society it is probably pointless to seek to eradicate all class (or gender) differences, but must this mean that the working class (or women) must inevitably play less overall?

Involvement in sport

In all the cities that we investigated, the working class was less strongly represented among the sports centre users that we sampled than in the general populations (see York et al, 1989). It is well-known that middle class adults are the more likely to be "in" sport, and our evidence shows that the working class adults who remained "in" tended to differ from middle class players in the amounts of money that they spent. So far there is a neat parallel with the male-female contrast. Thereafter, however, this parallel breaks-down, for in terms of their overall volume of sport activity there were only minor differences between the middle and working class players in our sample.

For the purposes of much of this analysis we have divided respondents into middle and working class groups using a combination of occupational and educational status. Individuals whose normal occupations were in the Registrar General's social classes one and two, the upper and intermediate non-manual grades, have been allocated to the middle class, while those in the manual grades or whose only labour market experience was of schemes or unemployment have been allocated to the working class. Respondents whose normal occupations were in the lower non-manual grades have been placed in the middle or working classes depending on whether they had remained in full-time education beyond age 16, and all individuals who were still in full-time education at the time of the research have been allocated to the middle class. This division of the sample is not meant to correspond with the main cleavage in the social structure, if there is such a division. Nor is it supposed to have any special significance for sport activity. It is simply a way of distinguishing respondents who were relatively privileged in socio-economic terms from those who were relatively disadvantaged.

When we compare the members of these two classes who were participating in sport to any extent in terms of our various measures of activity, the overall impression is of there being very few differences. When differences existed, these did not always indicate that the middle class had a privileged position in sport. For instance, in 1987 31 percent of the working class, but only 26 percent of the middle class participants were playing for more than eight hours per week in total. However, the middle class participants were the more likely to be playing four or more sports (25 percent compared with 16 percent). Between 1986 and 1987 almost identical proportions of the middle and working class players increased and reduced their sport activity, though between 1987 and 1988 the middle class respondents were the more likely to increase their participation (38 against 33 percent), while the working class participants were the more likely to report no change (25 and 18 percent).

Class differences in levels, and changes in sport activity tended to be widest among, or confined to women. Working and middle class male players had the more similar overall levels of sport activity and fidelity. The main class differences among the male players were in their particular sports and general "styles" of participation. The working class males were tending to spend less, but by playing fewer sports rather than by playing less overall. Playing fewer games left their sport careers slightly more vulnerable, but it appeared to be mainly the women players and non-participants who were paying most of the penalties of being working class. Overall the class differences within our sample of players were neither as strong nor as consistent as those associated with gender.

From our evidence it appeared that the working class males who survived in sport into adulthood in our survey areas were thereafter just as active as middle class players. The lower overall participation rate among working class adult males would have been due to their higher retirement rate in youth and young adulthood.

Table 4.1 gives the mean sport participation scores in 1987 for males and females according to their normal occupations, types of housing, employment status at the time of the enquiry, and income. Among the males there was no tendency for the lower status groups to play sport less. In fact the non-skilled working class players had a slightly higher mean participation score than the top professional and managerial group. Males who lived in council houses were playing slightly more sport than owner-occupiers, and the unemployed were playing more than full-time employees. Among the females, however, the differences in Table 4.1 generally favour the economically and occupationally privileged, though the figures show that the sex gap, with the social class indicators held constant, was consistently wider.

Table 4.1 also summarises the changes that occurred between 1987 and 1988 in the sport activity of the different occupational and employment groups. The data show that the sporting lives of the non-skilled working class, the unemployed and the housewives had been more vulnerable than among other groups. Social class was making no difference to the overall amounts of sport that male participants played in 1987, and little difference to female players' levels of activity. However, the economically disadvantaged

Table 4.1a *Sex, Class and Mean Participation Scores*

	Males	Females
	1987 (Players only)	
R/G Class		
1	57	42
2	46	36
3a	56	44
3b	57	36
4 & 5	60	36
Type of housing		
Owner-occupied	54	44
Privately rented	66	43
Council	62	39
Employment status		
Full-time	54	40
Part-time	63	39
Housewife	-	36
Unemployed	56	-
	1988 (Players only)	
Income		
< £2500	57	39
- £5000	46	32
- £7500	56	35
- £10,000	53	43
- £12,500	53	39
- £15,000	51	45
- £20,000	51	57

Table 4.1b *Mean Participation Scores Difference 1987-1988*

	Increasers Minus Decreasers
R/G Class	
1	– 4%
2	+1%
3a	– 9%
3b	+4%
4 & 5	–16%
Employment status (1988)	
Full-time	– 4%
Part-time	– 8%
Housewife	–22%
Unemployed	–27%

groups were the more likely to reduce their participation, sometimes dropping-out altogether, and, of course, they were the least likely to be in sport to begin with.

Social class in young adulthood

Our evidence suggests, by default to some extent since we did not study children, that class makes its most decisive impact on sport participation during the critical life-stages of childhood, youth and young adulthood. For a variety of reasons young people on middle class life courses are the most likely to be introduced to a wide range of sports, and to continue to participate throughout the years when sport careers are most vulnerable. Children in middle class families are often given flying starts in sport because their homes are the more likely to contain an abundance of equipment and sports-active parents. These young people tend to succeed academically in education, identify with their schools, and become willing participants in extra-curricula activities including sport (Hendry, 1978). They manage do do "a lot" with their time – schoolwork, homework, part-time jobs in many cases, plus a variety of sporting, cultural and social activities (Prosser, 1981). The evidence from our research suggests that they are then developing the skills of time management required to handle the rich but hectic leisure styles (see chapter ten) which many retain in later life. Other sports advantages of young people on middle class trajectories arise during the years immediately following compulsory education. Those with middle class ambitions and destinies stay-on and thereby retain privileged access to a wealth of heavily subsidised and often free (to students) sport facilities. These facilities are not only free or cheap to use, but conveniently located for students. Such advantages continue for those who progress into higher education where sport participation is the norm among males and females. Indeed, the sex gap in sport activity among students is narrower than among any other members of their age group (Furlong et al, 1989). Thereafter the highly educated can carry their sports interests into later life, and will normally live and work with peers among whom sport activity is normal.

Early school-leavers have none of these advantages. Neither employers nor youth training schemes have typically offered work-based recreation. Out-of-school youth must rely on community provisions including, in some areas, dual use of education-based facilities. Out-of-school youth's opportunities depend on what is available locally. Here there is considerable variation, but in terms of ease of access and cost they are normally hugely disadvantaged relative to full-time students. Hence their higher drop-out rate from sport. Only the most dedicated, mostly males, are likely to survive.

Attitudes

There were far more cross-class similarities than differences in our sample's attitudes towards sport. Indeed, there were hardly any class differences in the advantages seen in playing, or in the reasons given when individuals had increased their participation. The entire sample was generally agreed on the benefits of sport participation (enjoyment, fitness and social contact), the characteristics of a good sports centre, and so on.

Where there were class differences these suggested that middle class respondents were the more concerned about time. This was not because they had less leisure time than working class respondents, but because they had so many additional leisure interests. They were the more likely to name "time" as a disadvantage in playing sport (37 against 26 percent), and the middle class non-participants were by far the more likely to mention "more time" as a circumstance under which they might return (73 against 38 percent). Middle class respondents were also the most likely to give "time" reasons when they had reduced their participation (39 against 34 percent), and to give "travel" or "convenience" as the reasons when they had changed centres (41 against 32 percent). Other middle class emphases were that these players were the most likely to mention "health" (52 against 39 percent) and "relieving stress" (37 against 25 percent) as reasons for taking part in sport.

Money was often named as a disadvantage (by just under a third of the entire sample) but rarely as a barrier to individuals' own sport participation. There were no significant social class differences in this respect. Sport's time demands were obviously seen as the heaviest price, especially by middle class respondents. This was not just because they were typically working full-time in paid employment, but also, as indicated earlier, on account of their generally busy leisure lives (see chapter ten). If their time could somehow have been expanded, it is likely that their sport participation would have risen even higher. Working class respondents did not necessarily feel that they had literally spare time on their hands, but they seemed less inclined to return to sport or increase their participation if only their time budgets permitted.

Belfast

If it was not attitudes but, as argued earlier, their opportunities, access to facilities, particularly in childhood and youth, that was accounting for the persistence of social class inequalities in sport participation, how might providers respond to this situation? For a demonstration that sex equality was possible we can refer to Camden, and for proof that working class participation could reach and surpass typical middle class levels we can point to Belfast.

By the late-1980s inner-Belfast's rate of sport participation was higher than throughout the UK in general, social class inequalities were narrower, and even the city's unemployed had activity rates on a par with the general population's in mainland Britain (Roberts et al, 1989). Belfast did not have a long tradition of high sport participation. The explanation for the late-1980s situation lay in the 14 new, purpose-built sport and leisure centres that were opened between 1977 and 1984. These centres were not scattered throughout the city but were deliberately sited in areas of socio-economic deprivation, mostly in the inner-city where the residents found themselves surrounded by an extraordinary wealth of sports provision. These new facilities were built with central government cash. The unusual political situation in Northern Ireland explained central government's willingness to provide such support. However, there can surely be little doubt that similar levels of provision would be followed by similar levels of sport activity in other parts of the UK.

Belfast's new facilities were made accessible to inner-city residents in areas with high levels of unemployment and poverty, and a great deal of poor housing, not only by their siting (most districts were given their own centres) but also by keeping user charges low. In 1988 only 15 percent of the centres' running costs were being recouped from users compared with a typical recovery ratio of 50 percent in Britain at that time. Belfast's normal tariffs were modest, and generous concessions were available for groups such as the unemployed.

By the late-1980s in Belfast overall levels of sport participation were rising as a result of more young adults being retained, acquiring wide repertoires of skills and interests, then carrying their propensity to participate into later life-stages. Provisions for inner-Belfast's residents were generous compared with community facilities in most parts of the UK, but no more bountiful than the opportunities normally offered to students in higher education.

Belfast may represent one way, but it will not necessarily be the only way of closing class inequalities in sport. Public providers in other parts of the

UK tended to regard Belfast as an unhelpful and irrelevant case since, in the late-1980s, they could see no likelihood of being able to emulate its provisions. Does our evidence indicate ways of redistributing less generous public resources so as to raise working class sport activity to middle class levels?

Siting

Our research was designed to ascertain whether particular types of buildings or sports programmes, whether facilities were in the commercial, voluntary or public sectors, or the pricing or other management strategies were making any difference to the types of users. Far and away the best predictor of the users' class profile was a centre's siting. Forty-three percent of respondents in our facility surveys lived within two miles of the centres. This meant that the facilities in working class areas had the highest proportions of working class users, those in multi-racial areas had the most ethnic minority customers, and so on. The major centres in central city locations had the widest catchment areas and the most mixed user profiles. Location had no implications for the sex or age of the users, but it was making a considerable difference to their social class backgrounds. Even small "community" facilities were drawing some users from quite far afield. This was always occurring when sports centres' home teams had fixtures against visitors. It was also due to centres possessing instructors or equipment that enthusiasts with interests in weight training, martial arts or whatever considered superior to provisions at their nearest facilities. Other users were travelling to play with friends. However, every user survey ever conducted in the UK has found that local residents have been well-represented (Veal, 1985). This means, given the substantial residential class segregation that exists in the UK, that a sound strategy for increasing working class sport participation would be to site facilities in working class districts.

This had been the policy in Belfast. Elsewhere such positive discrimination was less pronounced. The reasons for this were partly practical and partly "political". Targeting was a recent fashion and, once built, facilities were fixed. There was simply no convenient way in which a local authority could re-site existing centres. In any case, residents and elected representatives from owner-occupied, mainly middle class districts were as able, probably more capable of lobbying for local sport facilities than inner-city dwellers and council estate tenants. Even committed local authorities have found it difficult to over-ride the lobbying and persuasiveness of privileged groups. Despite its rhetoric, the Greater London Council (1986) did not succeed in redistributing its leisure budget to favour its more disadvantaged boroughs (Tomlinson and Walton, 1986).

Sports

At the centres that we investigated there were certain sports, particularly bowls, martial arts and snooker, that had higher proportions of working class players than the other activities on which we focused, especially keep fit/ weight training and badminton. However, there seemed to be less scope for attracting members of specific social classes by sports programming than by siting.

Firstly, the relationships between sports and the players' social class backgrounds were rather weak. The middle class never amounted to more than 62 percent of all participants in any sport. All the sports were attracting substantial numbers of players from all social classes. Secondly, apart from very expensive sports, the relationships between particular games and social classes in the UK have arisen largely through historically specific circumstances. There is nothing inherent in the sports themselves to prevent the middle classes enjoying soccer, or the working classes playing rugby union. The entirely different class appeal of the latter game in England compared with Wales proves this point. Thirdly, it would be short-sighted to encapsulate working class interests and skills within the narrow range of sports to which such individuals had access in the past. Given the importance of broad-based foundations, a condition for extending participation among working class adults will be to widen young people's sports interests. And according to our evidence, particularly from Belfast, all that is likely to be required to increase working class participation in sports such as badminton and squash is to make these games available in working class areas.

Management

The actual and potential contributions of the commercial and voluntary sectors are discussed fully in chapter six. Suffice it to say here that whatever sector a centre belonged to was making less difference to the social class composition of its users than where it was sited, except that there was a general tendency for the public centres to have the highest proportions of users from economically disadvantaged groups such as the unemployed, and the working class more generally. Commercial provisions were rarely reaching non-employed adults – housewives and the retired as well as the unemployed. Nor was the commercial sector seeking or attracting many children. The main reason for the economically disadvantaged making the greatest use of public provisions was that all of the local authorities were making some special efforts to ensure that their facilities were accessible to the groups in question.

Nearly every centre that we visited, whatever the sector, practised differential pricing. Play was normally cheapest at off-peak times. Altogether 30 percent of the respondents in our facility surveys had paid less than the full rate: 32 percent in both the public and voluntary sectors and 24 percent in commercial premises. The likelihood of participants having benefited from concessionary prices varied by economic status: 59 percent of retired and 54 percent of sick and disabled users had paid less than the full rates. So had 45 percent of school pupils aged 16 and over, and 43 percent of the unemployed. Between 30 and 35 percent of college students, housewives, individuals with part-time occupations, and on the Youth Training Scheme and other employment measures were taking advantage of concessions, against just 23 percent of those with full-time jobs. The latter were eligible because cut-price play was sometimes available for all at off-peak hours. All non-employed groups were better-able than those with jobs, unless their hours of work were part-time or shifts, to take advantage of off-peak concessions. These were widely available in all sectors. However, public sector concessions tended to be the most generous, and groups such as the unemployed and the retired or over-50s were sometimes specially targeted. As explained in chapter two, they were eligible for reduced admission charges on top of any "normal" concessions in some districts, and (at restricted times) freesport in Liverpool. Qualifying sometimes required the production of a UB40 or pension book. An alternative administrative arrangement was to allow such groups to obtain passports or membership cards. Voluntary and commercial facilities were less able, or felt less need to display such generosity.

It is necessary to stress that there were huge variations in user profiles from centre to centre within all sectors, even within the same cities. Indeed, these contrasts were much wider than the aggregate differences between users of all commercial, voluntary and public facilities. In public centres that we surveyed within the same cities, the proportions of working class players ranged from nil to 61 percent in badminton, and of the unemployed from 5 to 77 percent in indoor soccer, and from nil to 25 percent in martial arts. Most of these differences were explicable in terms of the centres' local catchment areas, but others were obviously due to the managements' efforts to promote particular sports to target groups. Previous research has pointed to the many ways in which centre managements can shape their user profiles by active marketing and tailoring programmes to the interests and time schedules of particular sections of the population (Centre for Leisure Research, 1985; Griffiths and Veal, 1985). Blanket subsidies for participant sport have been heavily criticised for benefiting mainly the better-off who could afford to pay the full cost (Gratton, 1984; Gratton and Taylor, 1987). Chapter two explained that during the 1980s the local authorities in all our research areas had become more "selective" and pro-targeting. However, our evidence suggests that these kinds of social engineering were unlikely to remove all inequalities of opportunity.

Firstly, concessionary pricing was often attracting users who would have played in any case, sometimes at different times and places. Secondly, to take just one disadvantaged group, most unemployed users in our surveys were not benefiting from any concessions. Some preferred to participate at their normal times and with their normal companions. In other cases the individuals were unaware of the concessions, or felt that proving eligibility was not worth the hassle. Thirdly, even when former long-term non-participants were attracted to special sessions, their new careers in sport tended to be short-lived.

The normal structure of sport careers means that equalising opportunities for the exceptionally disadvantaged will depend on equalising opportunities throughout the larger sections of the population that are at risk of disadvantages such as unemployment at particular points in life. Pricing and sports programming could certainly assist, but our evidence suggests that siting was far more important. Indeed, appropriate siting was usually a precondition for other initiatives.

The volume of provision

The increased provisions for indoor sports since the 1960s may have created an impression, especially in non-users' minds, that the facilities now exist to make sport for all a reality and that the sole remaining task is to persuade the public to take advantage. This impression is gravely mistaken. Purpose-built, heavily subsidised, publicly-owned and managed sport and leisure centres, as in Belfast, may not be the sole or the most cost-effective way of providing for sport for all, but whoever does the providing there should be no doubt that someone will have to construct and run additional facilities.

In every city that we investigated, even where provision was most sparse, there was under-occupancy at off-peak times. Centre managements had been made to feel that under-use was a problem. There was pressure everywhere to increase throughput and revenue. Yet all leisure services carry spare off-peak capacity. This applies in shops, hotels, theatres, theme parks and holiday resorts. Leisure has to be catered for when consumer demand peaks. Even in the cities where provision was most generous there was unmet demand for accommodation in sports halls, squash courts and exercise rooms at peak hours. The replies to our questions on attitudes and motivations show that time was seen as a major cost and impediment to sport participation. If potential players could not be accommodated when *they* had the time, their interest was likely to be deflected into other leisure markets.

5

THE LIFE-COURSE

The main features of our sample's sport careers were summarised in chapter three: the heavy drop-out in youth and young adulthood, and the odds against individuals who quit soon after leaving school ever returning to sport compared with the loyalty of those who continued throughout their twenties and were then likely to play regularly for many more years. It was necessary to describe these broad outlines of typical sport careers so as to know where to look (mainly young adulthood) to uncover the roots of gender and social class inequalities. However, there is more to be said in qualification and amplification of the main trends in sport participation during the life course.

Suitable games

Our evidence shows that individuals who remained in sport into adulthood usually changed the games that they played. The age composition of participants varied considerably from sport to sport. According to the evidence from our facility surveys, types of centres (large or small, new or old, for example) did not have comparable age-specific appeals. Where a particular age group dominated a centre, this was invariably linked to the sports programme. For example, swimming was popular among children, so facilities with swimming pools usually had high proportions of child users. Particular sports were proving especially good at attracting and holding onto adult players, whereas, according to our evidence, neither the public, commercial nor voluntary sectors, nor large or small centres exerted equally focused appeals to particular age-bands. Drawing-in children and young people, and holding-on to players in their 40s and 50s, was proving feasible in all kinds of facilities, given appropriate sports programming.

Among the sports that we targeted in the facility surveys, swimming had the most bottom-heavy age profile. This activity had a widespread appeal to children of both sexes. Any pool, but particularly leisure pools, were liable to be used mainly by the under-16s unless children were deliberately excluded by pricing or management policies, which was most common in the commercial facilities that we studied. However, it would be misleading to label swimming as a children's pastime. The proportion of the population taking part declines with age, but swimming is the UK's most popular single sport in all age-groups if walking is excluded. It is an exceptional activity in attract-ing both sexes of all ages, and was often being retained as a primary or secondary form of physical recreation for as long as the members of our sample remained in any sport.

Among the sports on which we focused, martial arts, soccer and snooker were the activities in which older players were most heavily outnumbered by 16-24 year olds. These were examples of young adults' sports, especially young men's. Any centre that made extensive provision for these activities could rely on drawing-in substantial numbers of young people. Indeed, allowing a facility to be dominated by these sports, with or without swim-ming, easily created the ambience of a playground or youth club. Badminton, keep-fit sessions, weight training, and bowls had higher proportions of players aged 25-plus. Among the sports that we studied in detail, bowls had the most top-heavy age profile. This sport was proving exceptional not only in its specific appeal to people in middle age and beyond, but also in its ability to attract such individuals who had no prior experience of the game.

Managements in the centres that we studied knew that they could in-crease their numbers of adult users by offering suitable sports. Attracting particular age groups was known to require appropriate sports programming, and organisation also, because, as explained below, people's motivations and constraints were changing during the life course. Indeed, our evidence suggests that organisational style could be just as important as the sports programme in determining which age groups would dominate a centre because most sports which were being played into late adulthood were first played by the individuals concerned much earlier in their lives, and therefore also had an appeal within younger age-groups.

We explained in chapter three that the typical long-running sport career had involved some reconstruction every two or three years. Give-ups and take-ups had not normally coincided end-on. Particular games had not usually been dropped in order to concentrate upon, or to accommodate alternative sports. Chapter three also explained that there was a weak tendency for sports to have been given-up, temporarily or permanently, alongside other dislocating life events such as completing education, changing employment, marrying or separating, and moving house. Our evidence is not clear-cut on whether such life events had a negative impact across the sample's leisure in general. In chapter three we saw that that was a weak negative association between the number of life events that respondents had experienced between 1986 and 1988 and changes in their sport participation during that period. Fifty-two percent of the sample had experienced at least one life event between 1986 and 1988. In the 1988 interviews 24 percent of the sample claimed that their leisure had been affected by life events during the previous two years, and in 74 percent of these cases the claimed effect was withdrawal from or reduced participation in one or more activities. The relationships between our sample's sporting lives and other uses of leisure are discussed fully in section three. Suffice it to say here that in 1986 and

1988 we collected sufficient information to profile every respondent's general leisure style and to quantify his or her overall volume of leisure activity. According to these quasi-objective measurements, the greater the number of life events that individuals experienced between 1986 and 1988, the greater their likelihood of *increasing* their participation in non-sporting leisure. The indications were that life events were bad for sport but good for other kinds of leisure participation, though in each case the relationships were weak and fell short of statistical significance. In 1988 respondents might have been more sensitive about activities and friendships that had been lost rather than those they they had gained as a result of life events. However, the majority of those who experienced the events did not believe that their leisure had been affected either positively or adversely, and our objective evidence is consistent with this weight of opinion. Careers and patterns of participation in sport and other kinds of leisure seemed to have a momentum of their own which was resilient to changes in their occupational and domestic lives.

As pointed-out previously, take-ups and give-ups had both been common events in long-running sport careers. The effect of life events amounted to no more than a slight increase in the normal tempo of give-ups. Take-ups seemed even less affected, and it was in the course of such normal adjustments in their sporting lives that players had moved gradually from predominantly children's and young people's sports into other games. However, take-ups in adulthood were mostly of sports that the individuals had learnt to play earlier in life. There was no sudden replacement of young people's sports by adult activities in the typical long-term sport career. Rather, sports that appealed mainly to young people had been phased down gradually, while formerly secondary sports were elevated into the individuals' primary activities. Alongside these changes in their sports, the players' motivations, and the constraints to which they were exposed, were also changing gradually.

Motivations and constraints

Age differences here were mostly marginal, as between the sexes and social classes. Even so, the differences indicate that younger and older players were seeking rather different satisfactions, and were most likely to take part in sport under rather different conditions (see also Rudman, 1989).

In all age groups the main reasons given when respondents had increased their sport activity were that they enjoyed it, to keep fit, and to improve their standards. However, the older age groups were the least likely to name latter benefit. Answers to other questions also indicated that the older they grew, the less concerned did players become about improving their performances. For example, the proportions giving raising their standards of play as a reason for participating declined from 37 percent among 16-24 year olds to 29 percent among the over-45s, while the proportions giving "performance" answers as an advantage of playing declined from 54 percent to 41 percent. The older participants seemed less interested in proving to themselves or to anyone else that they could become more proficient. They were discovering other satisfactions in sport. There was less emphasis on competition and standards in the over-45s' motivations, and more appreciation of the social benefits. The "opportunity to mix" was given as a reason for playing by 80 percent of the over-45 year old participants against 55 percent of those aged 16-24.

There was certainly no general feeling that sport was inappropriate for older people. The proportions who saw absolutely no disadvantages in playing sport actually rose from 45 percent among 16-24 year olds to 67 percent among the over-45s. And the older respondents were the most likely to name the middle-aged as people who were particularly likely to benefit (56 percent compared with 39 percent of 16-24 year olds).

The older the age-group, the more prominent did social aspects become in respondents' sport motivations, and lack of health and fitness became increasingly prominent among their perceived obstacles to sport activity. The proportions of those who reduced their participation who gave "poor health" as a reason rose from 15 percent to 27 percent with age, and the proportions of non-players who named "better health" as a condition for resuming sport rose from 13 percent to 50 percent. The older respondents felt more restricted by their physical condition, but were less likely than the younger age-groups to name time and money as constraints. The proportions mentioning the cost as a disadvantage in playing sport fell from 40 percent to 22 percent with age. Among the non-participants, the proportions listing a need for "more money" as a condition for resuming their sport careers fell from 23 to 13 percent. Also, the proportions of non-participants who said that they would play if they had more time fell from 59 percent among 16-24 year olds to 25 percent among the over-45s. The older age-groups were the least likely to regard time as a constraint on their own participation, and were the most likely to name "filling time" as an actual advantage of sport activity (38 percent of the over-45s compared with 27 percent of 16-24 year old players).

The evidence illustrates how, with advancing age, players were tending to change not only the sports that they played, but also their motivations and styles of participation. The constraints on their leisure were changing. Individuals became more likely to feel restricted by their personal health and fitness, and less anxious to improve their sport performances. Time and money became less restricting, and individuals became more sensitive to the social benefits of sport activity. Catering for older age groups, therefore, was not just a matter of offering the right sports, but also of creating an appropriate atmosphere in which opportunities to socialise were prominent, and in which there was less emphasis on winning or even improving.

Marginal players

In chapter three we drew attention to the polarisation of the UK's adult population in terms of sport activity. On the one side, a minority have continuous careers and typically play several sports during all periods in their adult lives. We demonstrated the high probability of individuals who stayed loyal to sport throughout their twenties continuing to play regularly for many more years. On the other side, there are many who lapse from sport in youth or young adulthood and are then unlikely ever to return on a regular basis whatever the quality and however strenuously local facilities are marketed. Thirty-four percent of the non-participants in our sample said that "nothing" would encourage them to resume sport. Most of these "outsiders" had long histories of abstinence, and, in so far it errs, we suspect that our 34 percent figure will under-estimate the proportion of non-participants in the general adult population who were very unlikely to return to sport.

Chapter three also drew attention to an intermediate group, amounting to around a quarter of all sport participants at any time, who had moved into and out of participation, sometimes repeatedly, during their adult lives. Such interrupted careers are not inconsistent with our polarisation thesis since they were a smaller group than either of the others. Our facility surveys showed that among those using sport provisions at any point in time, individuals with continuous careers were in the majority. Simultaneously, the number of confirmed abstainers in the local adult populations would have exceeded the numbers who were moving into and out of participation in sport.

The ways in which our sample's interrupted sport careers had developed did not differ fundamentally from the continuous players'. Both groups had dropped or taken-up a sport on average once for every two or three years of participation. Only a minority of the players maintained stable sport behaviour over the 12 month period between our 1987 and 1988 surveys. Fifty-five percent of the participants in 1987 recorded different participation scores in 1988. Change had been a normal feature of both continuous and discontinuous sport careers. What made the crucial difference was that the discontinuous careers tended to lack depth. The individuals concerned had held fewer sports in their repertoires from youth onwards, and during their participation phases they often played just one sport. So whenever they gave up an activity, temporarily or permanently, their entire participation often lapsed. The continuous players were mostly involved in several sports on a regular basis every year, and were therefore able to reconstitute their careers without lapsing altogether. The women in our sample had a higher proportion of interrupted, and a smaller proportion of continuous careers than the men because the females' involvement in sport was generally shallower.

In earlier chapters we emphasised the importance of facilities in determining whether or not different groups of young people would develop the broad repertoires of sports interests and skills that were likely to sustain long-term careers. Facilities also appeared to be playing a role in determining how many adults remained in sport. The adult players in our sample had repeatedly changed both the sports in which they were active, and the centres at which they played indoor games. According to our evidence, in the late 1980s around 15 percent of continuous players, that is, not including those who moved into or out of sport altogether, were changing the centres at which they played during any 12 month period. Established players were often testing out different centres in pursuit of the best conditions, or to accompany old or new playing companions. Other movements had been due to new and often more convenient facilities becoming available.

Our evidence suggests the adults who had become locked into sport were normally finding somewhere to play however sparse the provisions in the areas where they had settled, and whatever the other demands on their time. In contrast, marginal players, typically with discontinuous careers, could be held or lost to sport depending on the facilities that were currently available in their areas. Whether their careers in sport remained alive could hinge on their access to local centres, teams and clubs that were suitable given their age, sex and sports interests. Now there were enough marginal players in the local adult populations in our research areas for increased or upgraded provisions to make an immediate impact on levels of participation in all age groups, but this does not contradict our insistence that there were richer long-term gains to be made by expanding the pools of young adults who were embarking on either continuous or interrupted careers.

Later-life revival

We emphasised in chapter three that the retirement rate from sports was steepest in young adulthood within our sample, as throughout the wider population. Our evidence shows that the give-up rate then declined rapidly, and from the mid-20s onwards more slowly, to become miniscule in the 60-plus age group. Take-ups of sports had also been most common in young adulthood – the life-phase when individuals were experimenting and widening their ranges of leisure skills and interests. Thereafter, within our sample, the sport take-up rate per year subsided, like the give-up rate, but with a crucial difference that the take-up rate declined only until individuals were aged 40-50, then rose marginally. Up to age 40-50 the number of sport give-ups per year exceeded the number of take-ups in our sample. Hence the gradual movement out of sport with advancing age. However, from age 50 onwards the take-up rate exceeded the give-up rate, indicating a net increase in sport participation. These trends in our sample's give-up and take-up rates are described in Figure 5.1.

Surveys of the general population are unlikely to highlight this trend because the number of sport players aged 50-plus, even in large samples, will usually be too small to allow fine distinctions according to levels and trends in sporting habits. According to our evidence, the rise in participation at 45-plus was mostly within the pool who had remained in touch with sport through earlier life-phases, and most of the increase was due to these participants displaying more loyalty than younger age-groups. Our evidence shows that sport in later life had a rather different style than in younger

Figure 5.1

Age-Specific Give-up and Take-up Rates
(all sports)

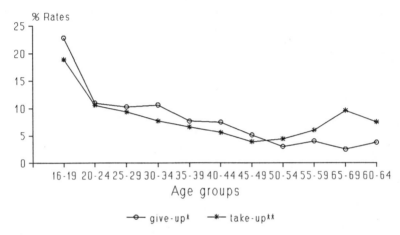

—⊖— give-up*   —*— take-up**

*Years 'at risk' with at least one sport
give-up
**Years with at least one sport take-up

adults' recreation. The players aged 45-plus in our sample displayed exceptional stability in the sports that they played, and in their frequency of participation from year to year (see also Mihalik et al, 1989). Between 1986 and 1988 they were less likely either to increase or reduce their activity than younger participants. We have already explained that the older players had rather different motivations. They placed more stress on the social benefits than younger players, and were less concerned to improve their standards. Also, the participants aged 45-plus were typically playing fewer sports than the younger players. It was far more common in the older age-groups for individuals to be active in solitary sports. However, they tended to play their retained sports with above-average frequency, so their total volume of participation was not far short of younger age groups' levels.

Another difference in their style of participation was that on average the older players were spending less. This would have been another reason, apart from many possessing more disposable income than in earlier life-stages, for the older age groups being less conscious of the cost as a disadvantage and obstacle to playing sport. The average 16-24 year old player in our sample was spending £3.80 per week on membership fees, admissions, travel and journals. In the 55-plus age group the average outlay on these items was just

£1.60. This difference was only partly due to the over-55s playing less frequently. They tended to have fewer sports, which reduced their outlays on membership fees, and the older players were tending to avoid relatively expensive sports such as martial arts and snooker. Individuals who had retired from paid employment often played at off-peak times at concessionary rates, and additional concessions were sometimes available at sessions aimed specifically at the over-50s. This meant that even when they played the same amounts of sport, on average the over-50s were spending less than 25-44 year olds.

For the remainder of the twentieth century the number of young adults in the UK will decline. This will be an inevitable result of the downward trend in the birth-rate in the 1970s. For several decades into the twenty-first century the proportion of the population in the older age groups will increase – an inescapable product of the relatively high birth-rates from the 1940s until the 1960s, combined with our increased chances of survival into very old age. These trends mean that unless sport broadens its appeal and becomes less dependent on the younger age groups, overall levels of participation per head of population in the UK are almost certain to fall. Sport has a vested interest in the potentially buoyant market in the 45-plus age group where increasing numbers are experiencing a lightening of family responsibilities and disengaging from their main occupational careers while still facing 30 or more years of active life. Many are reasonably prosperous as well as physically and mentally agile. The 45-plus age-group is a major source of the new leisure connoisseurs – individuals who become keenly interested and often extremely knowledgeable in their chosen fields. Sport can be among the latter, though according to our evidence, the size of the participant sport market in later life is heavily governed by the number of adults who remain in contact throughout earlier life-stages.

Persuading more older citizens to stay-in sport will depend on keeping younger careers alive, and also upon making appropriate provisions for older players. This will mean offering the right sports, in the style that older players tend to prefer. And sport will face fierce competition for this age group's time and spending. This is the case at all life-stages, but at 45-plus the competition is likely to be especially intense since the benefits that actual and potential sport players seek, particularly the sociability, are available in many other leisure activities.

Divisions

Sport players are a far from united body. We found that they tended to stick with their own crowds – their sessions, partners, clubs and teams. They were divided by the games that they played, the centres and sessions that they attended, and, simultaneously in many instances, by age, sex, and often social class and ethnicity.

According to our evidence, most sport centres do not attract a particular type of user. The main exceptions among the centres that we surveyed were commercial facilities and voluntary sector clubs that were catering for single sports. Elsewhere it tended to be the sport session that was drawing a particular kind of person – male or female, and young or old, for example, who would also be united by their common interest in the activity. Players normally travelled to the centres either alone or in the company solely of the other people that they intended to play with. In our facility surveys we encountered few examples of friends or family groups arriving together in order to separate to play different sports. Most participants arrived at the facilities shortly before their sessions commenced and the majority left immediately afterwards. Any socialising at the centres was usually brief and confined to fellow-players. Lounge, cafeteria and bar facilities in the sports centres often resembled railway waiting rooms with a variety of groups passing through without anyone settling and with little intermingling. Most of the exceptions were in centres where the bars and social areas attracted their own clients, or in specialised commercial and voluntary centres where the users were relatively homogeneous in terms of age, sex and social class.

Sport was not integrating its participants into "society" at large, or even into a general sports-loving public. Most participants' strongest attachments in sport were to players of their own games, and who belonged to the same clubs or teams. Rather than drawing all activists together, sport was tending to splinter its participants. This is why the everyday "politics" of sport is less of a united campaign for more resources for all than a competition for time and space (see Jaakson, 1989). In this kind of situation the weakest, the least organised and committed, are the most likely to be squeezed-out unless someone with the necessary power exercises positive discrimination.

The next chapter discusses the implications of the different kinds and levels of provision for sport in the six areas that we studied for local levels and trends in participation between 1986 and 1988. This leads to conclusions about the types of provision that are most likely to deliver sport for all. However, the evidence already presented enables us to see why no single type of centre or management was likely to prove best for delivering sport to all sections of the populations in our survey areas, or throughout the country in general.

Overall levels of participation in the areas that we studied were more likely to be maximised by pluralism and diversity so that different sessions and even centres could be colonised by groups defined by various combinations of age, sex, social class, ethnicity and sports interest. Competitive swimmers did not wish to mingle with recreational bathers. Self-styled "serious" fitness addicts often displayed contempt for the equipment and regimes in centres that attracted the less dedicated. Maximising participation required catering for all tastes, which was more likely to mean keeping different sections of the sports public apart than blending them together.

6

THE IMPACT OF PROVISIONS

Trends in the six cities

Chapter two described the facilities for indoor sport in each of our cities, and explained how and why the local councils' policies were re-formulated in the late-1980s. Would the "new look" for public leisure services lead to changes in levels of use of the facilities or in the types of users? A good basis for prediction is the ways in which the changes in provision that occurred during our research impacted or, more accurately, failed to impact immediately on the local populations' sport behaviour.

Our findings are pessimistic on the likelihood of supply side changes making a strong and quick impression on either the overall level of sport activity or the types of people who take part. Provisions in each of the cities that we studied were unique in many respects, but as explained in chapter two, Liverpool, Glasgow and Cardiff were the places where new centres opened and, in this sense, facilities for indoor sport expanded most visibly during our research. In each of these cities the expansion was due to the local councils' efforts. The councils in Belfast, Camden and Chester were certainly not inactive, but they made no major additions to their local facilities during our fieldwork. Developments in these areas took the form of consolidation, upgrading and endeavouring to obtain better value from existing premises.

In terms of the public's sport behaviour in the cities, the only clear difference, according to the evidence from our samples, was that Camden was outstanding however the trends were measured. Table 6.1 summarises some of our relevant findings. It gives the proportions of the local samples who increased, minus those who decreased their sport activity (in terms of total participation scores) between 1987 and 1988. Camden was the place where respondents were the most likely to increase, and the least likely to reduce their frequency of participation. It was also the area whose sample was the most likely to add to, and the least likely to reduce the number of sports that they played, and where initial non-participants were most likely to take-up sport during 1988.

It would be tempting to conclude that upgrading and management efforts to achieve higher throughput in existing facilities were making a sharper impact on public behaviour than increasing the number of sport centres, except that trends in the Camden sample set them apart not just from respondents in the cities where facilities had increased, but in Belfast and Chester also. There were no clear differences between the other five cities. The rank order in terms of whether sport activity had increased or decreased changed according to the indicators, except that Camden always headed the list. The only clear and consistent contrast was between Camden and the rest. Overall there was no obvious fit between trends in provision in the six areas, and short-term changes in the local samples' sport behaviour.

Table 6.1 *Trends in the six cities; Increasers minus Reducers (1987-1988)*

| | Social class | | | Sex | | Age | | | |
	Total	MC	WC	M	F	-24	-34	-44	Older
Camden	+23	+8	+45	+24	+20	+10	0	+66	+16
Glasgow	-3	-15	+8	0	+1	-9	-2	-7	+3
Belfast	-2	+5	-11	+3	-6	-4	+5	+17	-22
Liverpool	-7	+1	-12	+6	-15	-1	-12	-7	0
Cardiff	-20	-17	-24	-6	-26	-27	-34	-18	-3
Chester	-12	-11	-13	-13	-11	-13	-13	-14	-13

Now the home addresses of our sample from the Camden sport facilities covered a much wider geographical area than in any other city. Many "Camden" respondents lived in other parts of the South-East but worked in or near central London. Camden residents themselves could easily cross borough boundaries in search of recreation. In our view, the rise in sport activity within the Camden sample is more likely to have been a product of the capital city's economic buoyancy in the mid to late-1980s, coupled with the dense conglomeration of recreational opportunities in London, than the leisure policies and provisions of Camden Borough Council itself.

Chapter two explained that, at the time of our fieldwork, targeting was still embryonic in all six cities. All the local authorities had measures intended to attract certain groups such as women, the over-50s and the unemployed, though the particular sectors of the public that were targeted, and the degree of effort varied from place to place. These variations in effort were not reflected in our samples' behaviour. In Camden all socio-demographic groups, not just those targeted by the council, were part of the relatively positive trend in sport activity from 1987 to 1988. Men and women in all age groups, and from the working and middle classes, were more likely to increase or less likely to reduce their participation in Camden than in any of the other cities. In Liverpool there were no signs of economically disadvantaged groups deriving exceptional benefits, relative either to other local residents or to their counterparts in the other cities, as a result of their council's relatively generous "freesport" policy.

We noted in chapter four that Camden had discovered, when monitoring use of its facilities in 1989, that men and women were equally represented. This was not due to any exceptional efforts by the local authority to target and attract women into sport. Liverpool's efforts on behalf of women had been more co-ordinated and thorough. The situation in Camden was more likely to have arisen through the local force of demand for aerobics and other forms of exercise generated by the number of women working and living in central London.

We appreciate that these conclusions clash with the experiences of sport centre managers who know that they can increase use by women, the unemployed, the over-50s or whoever by appropriate programming and publicity. Close and detailed monitoring of such initiatives appears to show that the efforts succeed. However, the findings from our research can be squared with this apparently contradictory evidence when account is taken, firstly, of the likelihood of special programmes drawing participants from other places, secondly that the impact of initiatives based on particular sessions and centres will amount only to a drop in the ocean of participation, and thirdly the high lapse rate among new players.

In the short-term, the main effects of increased or enhanced sport provisions seem to be to widen the choice and improve the facilities for established players. The immediate benefits of increasing or improving the stock of facilities, whether locally or nationally, flow mainly to individuals who would otherwise have played elsewhere. Our evidence on sport careers suggests that adults who are locked-in find somewhere to play however sparse the local facilities. If purpose-built centres are not available, they flood into schools, colleges and community halls. Conversely, when better facilities are provided established players are the quickest to respond and remain.

However, it would be a mistake to extrapolate our evidence on trends in sport behaviour over just one year to conclude that provisions make little or no *long-term* difference to levels and patterns of participation. A classic method of assessing the impact of planned social changes is the quasi-experimental study in which the relevant population is studied before and after a change is introduced, preferably as close to each side of the event as possible so as to reduce the possibility of other changes contaminating the results. The implication of our evidence on the structure of sport careers is that this methodology will systematically under-estimate and is likely to misrepresent the eventual effects of changes in provision. Chapter five explained why, in the short-term, the effects of supply-side changes in sports provision on public behaviour are likely to be marginal. This marginal difference is most

Figure 6.1

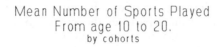

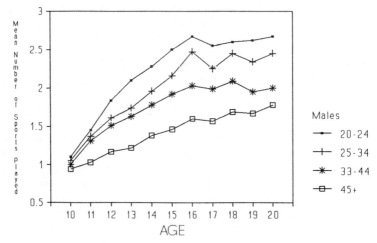

(includes years not played.)

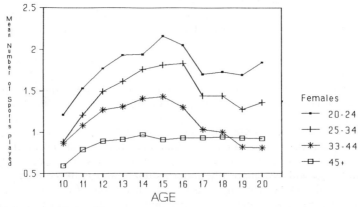

(includes years not played.)

likely to be made to vulnerable sport careers, when individuals are retained or lost depending on what is available locally. In the short-term these effects will normally make little impression on overall participation rates. In the longer-term, however, persistent marginal changes are guaranteed to make a more substantial impact on the overall level of participation and the types of people involved. By the late-1980s Belfast was beginning to experience the effects of the building programme completed between 1977 and 1984 (Roberts et al, 1989), whereas studies of sport participation throughout Northern Ireland in the early 1980s found it difficult to discern any effects whatsoever (McAuley and Hirons, no date). The impact was specific to the parts of Belfast where provisions had increased, and began to unwind only as increasing proportions of successive cohorts of young people carried their higher propensity to participate into adulthood.

Figure 6.1 compares the mean number of sports that the members of our sample played regularly at every age from 10 to 20, sub-divided by sex and age at the time of the research. In chapter three we explained that the number of sports played when young was the best predictor of whether individuals would continue to play into adulthood. Hence the significance of the information in Figure 6.1. The graphs show that young males in all the cohorts had played more sports than the young females. This adds to our evidence in chapter four: whatever the indicators selected, males were always the more heavily involved in sport. However, Figure 6.1 also shows that among both males and females the mean number of sports played when they were teenagers had risen progressively from the oldest to the youngest cohort. We had not expected to find such clear differences given that the older respondents in our sample were mainly the exceptional members of their age group who had remained in sport.

The only plausible explanation of the upward trend is that over time young people in all the areas had been given more opportunities to play a wide range of sports. This would have been due to developments in provisions for the community in general and in education. And this will be the most likely source of the gradual increase over time in adult participation rates throughout the country. Such an increase is the delayed but, according to our evidence, reliable by-product of introducing higher proportions of successive cohorts of young people to a wide range of sports. If provisions continue to increase in the future, and if even more young people are introduced to many sports, we are confident that the adult participation rate will also continue on its upward course. This vindicates the liberalisation of the physical education curriculum in schools. The trend towards broader programmes based on optional sport experiences has been criticised because the number and quality of teachers has often been insufficient to maintain standards hitherto expected. Nevertheless, the trend will have been in the right direction for raising adult sport participation.

In the short term, according to our evidence, it is the structure of demand – particularly the number and types of people with established sport careers

– that patterns adult participation. In the longer-term, however, our evidence suggests that the structure of demand responds to provisions. These, according to our own and other evidence, make their decisive impact during the critical life stages of childhood, youth and young adulthood. Furthermore, our evidence gives clear pointers to the types of provisions that are most likely to attract and retain marginal players during these crucial life stages. They want clean and friendly centres, with good changing rooms and equipment. They also want facilities that are close to their homes and which are easy to book at convenient times. Meeting young people's demands will depend on there being sufficient accommodation to offer a wide variety of sports appealing to both sexes, and enough space to satisfy other age groups, and elite performers without excluding those with more casual approaches and less sporting talent. Our evidence suggests that increased provisions will not merely be necessary to permit, but will actually produce rising levels of adult sport activity, given the advantages that virtually all citizens perceive in this type of recreation, though only in the long-term.

Hence the cause for concern that, at the time of our research, the local councils were becoming more obsessed with the short-term. They were under pressure to reduce unit costs quickly, partly as a result of general financial restraints and partly by the need to be in shape for CCT. Also, the Audit Commission had recommended monitoring effectiveness and strategy reviews at least every five years. The aim was not to force local councils to abandon, but to become more efficient and effective in pursuing social objectives. Would the Audit Commision have given the same advice had it realised that the most efficient and effective sports promotion is long-term, and that it may be necessary to wait a generation for monitoring to capture the full consequences?

Sectors

Chapter two explained that the local councils were the dominant influences on indoor sport provision in all six areas, and that at the time of our research these major providers were on the verge of a major change: they were preparing for compulsory competitive tendering (CCT). When first announced this legislation was not welcomed by the public sector leisure professions (Leisure Management, 1988), but subsequently many senior managers became enthusiastic. They embraced the change for the opportunity to shake-up their organisations, to specify objectives clearly, and to become more professional and cost-effective (Bacon, 1990). Throughout the UK, the standard response of local authorities to central government policies in the 1980s was to develop more market-oriented services (Henry, 1990). This was certainly the case in our research areas where preparing for CCT meant dividing the departments into client and contractor units, and cutting costs, which usually meant reducing staff. Most of the departments were confident that their in-house bids would succeed. Some of the local authorities had become experienced in fighting-off competitor bids for other services. The leisure services departments had inside knowledge, and some of them neither intended nor expected the contracts that they were drafting to tempt many commercial operators. Even if outside bids succeeded, the departments believed that the terms of the contracts would protect their existing ranges of services and social objectives.

However, our evidence suggests that it will be difficult to effect a large-scale transfer between the public and commercial sectors while leaving the services themselves intact. The initial phase of our survey work was spread across 18 public, 19 voluntary and 9 commercial sport facilities in order to assess whether these sectors differed consistently in their efforts and ability to attract various sections of the population. Here the differences were minor overall, though potentially crucial for certain groups including children, young people and the economically disadvantaged. And our findings also expose the mistake of imagining that the different sectors are simply alternative channels for meeting the same kinds and levels of recreational demand. What they were delivering was qualitatively different. Moreover, the sectors were driven by different "engines", which made it dangerous to assume that cut-backs in one sector would automatically produce compensating responses from the others (see Roberts et al, 1987).

Commerce was being driven by the engine of profitability. It catered for whatever demands appeared to be profitable. If a service ceased to be profitable, it ceased to be provided. The corporations and entrepreneurs in charge of the commercial centres that we investigated were involved in sport only while this business continued to make money. If alternative uses of their premises looked more profitable, sport would be deserted.

The presence of numerous private businesses in every city that we studied proves that extensive public and voluntary provisions were not making sport non-commercial. Private enterprise can always co-exist alongside subsidised or even free public provisions by offering superior services, if not outlawed entirely. This has occurred in health and education throughout the UK, but it was not the niche that most of the commercial sports centres that we visited had carved in their local markets. Commercial snooker and fitness clubs were competing successfully with public and voluntary provisions primarily by catering for specialised tastes. Commercial snooker was normally offered in snooker-only clubs, while exercise was available in specialist health and fitness studios. To the uninitiated it may have seemed that these latter enterprises were offering much the same service, but in fact different clubs were promoting different methods of achieving, and sometimes different conceptions of fitness. Sometimes snooker and exercise were being offered in hotel or nightclub environments where the total recreational experiences were rather different than could be obtained at local authority centres. So the commercial enterprises were attracting some clients who simply could not envisage themselves using public facilities. Markets tend to force competing businesses to target specific sections of the population by offering specialised wares. This happens in housing, publishing, restaurants, and sport also. Commercial sport is "different" in providing environments dedicated to particular interests, and which usually attract particular sections of the public defined by age, sex and socio-economic status (see Roberts et al, 1988). The commercial facilities that we surveyed were attracting individuals who wished to see themselves, and sometimes to be regarded as "the types" who belonged in the places in question.

The public centres that we studied were governed by rather different pressures. The managers knew that they were expected to serve all sections of the public. Hence their preference for balanced sport programmes. Domination by particular cliques was considered a problem. This is why there was "space" within the cities that we investigated for commerce to appeal to individuals with specialised interests who preferred to play in dedicated environments. Commerce was not always attracting the most serious and committed players. Some of the latter preferred the more open atmospheres in public centres and did not wish to be thought of as any "particular types" of persons.

All the commercial centres that we investigated were operating membership systems, though the members in no way controlled the clubs. The upfront payment was a strategy for restricting access to the committed and excluding anyone who did not appear "the right type". Casual use was possible at most of the commercial facilities, but it was not available automatically, and the membership systems enabled the managements to ensure that regulars had access to the facilities at their own convenience. No public centre was attempting to operate in this manner. Our evidence confirms what everyone senses from personal experience; commercial leisure is different. In commercial markets the consumer is sovereign; providers are pressured to offer services and facilities tailored to different individuals' and groups' wants.

Voluntary organisations are driven not by profit but by their members' enthusiasm which can be a powerful engine (Bishop and Hoggett, 1986). The history of sport is proof that people can be induced to push themselves to their limits for non-financial rewards. Most teams, clubs and leagues have always been run by amateurs. Such voluntary work has to be its own reward. There are special satisfactions in working without the pressures that accompany pay, and in earning the appreciation of others. These are the rewards that sustain volunteers' enthusiasm.

As explained in chapter two, sport facilities were being provided by several types of voluntary organisations in the areas that we studied. Firstly, there were sports associations that existed primarily to promote their particular games and to serve their own members but which were sometimes making their premises available for use by the wider community. Secondly, there were organisations dedicated to the welfare of particular groups such as young people which included sport among their services. Thirdly, there were organisations such as churches whose primary objectives had no necessary connection with sport, but whose premises were being made available for use by sports teams and clubs. Fourthly, in some of the areas voluntary associations had been brought into existence specifically to take-over privatised leisure centres. All these types of organisations shared in common only their voluntary foundations, which meant that the provisions could remain afloat only while volunteers were willing to take responsibility. The conditions on which this willingness rested are strictly beyond the scope of our analysis, but they did not include the desire of public authorities to increase or diminish their own contributions (Bishop and Hoggett, 1986).

Partnership between the public, commercial and voluntary sectors is as old as modern sport. Most playing fields and indoor facilities have always been publicly provided, whereas the equipment and clothing used in play have invariably been commercially produced and marketed. The teams, leagues, referees and coaches using public facilities have nearly always been organised by voluntary sports associations. Grant-aid has an equally long history. The boundaries between sectors can be blurred and may be invisible to players. The respondents in our facility surveys were often uncertain and disinterested in whether the centres that they were using were under voluntary or public ownership and management. Sports clubs that had opened their facilities to the general public were sometimes operating on commercial lines, and it was often difficult to tell whether a particular martial arts group or excercise class was part of a voluntary movement or a commercial venture of the leaders. Public centres recently contracted to commercial or voluntary management are not the first instances of facilities with an ambiguous status.

Despite this, our evidence suggests that none of the sectors is capable of fully emulating another's role. Neither local authorities nor commercial enterprises can routinely call upon the freely given effort on which voluntary associations run. Equally, neither the commercial nor voluntary sectors are likely to take-on the public sector's entire role because public provisions have been generated by very different processes (Coalter, 1986). There has never been just one reason for public sector involvement in participant sport. Local councils and national agencies have subsidised sport for a wide variety of purposes. These have included national and local prestige, encouraging socially acceptable uses of leisure time, promoting health and fitness, and providing recreational opportunities for groups that would otherwise be deprived. These motives share in common only that none automatically generates a commercial or voluntary response.

There may be socio-political or economic justifications for limiting the public sector's role in sport, but if the goal is to maximise participation, the obvious strategy will be to encourage each sector to do as much as it can of what it does best. In some ways they compete, but the different sectors also feed off each other. The history of sport in Britain illustrates how voluntary associations can thrive on grant aid and public facilities in which to play. Profitable opportunities in sport increase the higher the proportion of the population with wide-ranging sports interests and skills. The sectors' different contributions, and the division of labour between them that has developed in the UK in the past, mean that restricting the role of public provision will be less likely to kindle commercial and voluntary effort, in the short-term at any rate, than to weaken the supports on which their own provisions rest. Operating in parallel, the sectors can support each other and offer a wider variety of provisions that any single branch of the industry could supply. Fuelling all the engines will be the best strategy for maximising participation, and for creating the variety of facilities that will enable all sections of the sports-active public to claim their own time and space without crowding-out others.

Buildings

Our research was designed to allow us to compare the drawing power of different kinds of centres within sectors – large and small, wet and dry, purpose-built and converted, and dedicated mainly to sport as opposed to being available for many uses. Here our evidence shows that the type of user depended far more on a centre's siting and sports programme than the kind of building.

Our evidence does not suggest that the manner in which the UK's local authorities have developed facilities since the 1960s has been misguided. If they had possessed all the information now available at the outset, they would no doubt still have aimed for the mixtures of neighbourhood and major facilities that were typical at the time of our research. Our evidence explains why this will be the best recipe for maximising participation. Neighbourhood provisions are important because of the tendency for people to play close to their homes. The compensating advantage of large centres is well-known – the throughput that they generate results in relatively low unit costs (Scottish Sports Council, 1979). Major centres do not simply bring prestige: they are usually good buys on strict financial criteria. Also, major centres are needed to accommodate a wide range of sports. Smaller neighbourhood facilities are invariably limited in what they can offer. They are typically dry, and may not contain full-size sports halls.

Irrespective of size, our findings suggest that sports centres need to be high quality if they are to retain marginal players such as the young women who still desert sport in droves, though it is not only females who want good, clean accommodation in which to play and change; the men in our sample had exactly the same priorities. All the cities that we studied had discovered that as new sports centres opened, older facilities such as traditional swimming pools suffered a decline in custom. In sport, as in other spheres of modern life, there seems to be an inescapable spiral of rising expectations. If more people are to be retained in sport, therefore, they will have to be offered accommodation of the same standard as is available for their home-based and other out-of-home leisure. The councils in our survey areas had discovered that centres built in the 1960s and 70s were becoming shabby and needed upgrading by the 1980s. Hence the drive to improve changing rooms, to leisurise pools, and to add saunas and fitness suites.

Some of the local authorities had decided that the best way to expand their stocks of sports facilities rapidly was to build cheaply, to open more schools and colleges for dual use, and to use community halls. In the longer-term, however, we suspect that the councils that were investing in high quality buildings will reap the greater rewards. Whatever their size, we believe that sport facilities will need to be high quality relative to rising general expectations and standards if overall participation is to rise, especially in those sections of the population that, up to now, have been the most difficult to retain.

Sports

Our evidence shows that the case for making a wide range of sports available to players in all areas is over-determined given the goal of maximising participation. Firstly, individuals are most likely to remain in sport as adults if they are introduced to many games when young. Secondly, the different sexes and age groups tend to play different sports, which means that sport for all is unlikely to be achieved by promoting the same basic diet for everyone. Thirdly, our sample's continuous sport careers had typically involved repeated movements from game to game. Hence our suspicion that the strength of the Camden sample's sporting lives relative to trends in the other cities between 1987 and 1988 had less to do with the character or management of the facilities offered by Camden Council itself than the conglomeration of opportunities available to inner-London residents and workers. Certainly the full range of games played in our respondents' longer-term sport careers had rarely been catered for in single facilities.

Table 6.2 describes the trends between 1987 and 1988 in our sample's involvement in the seven sports on which we focused initially. The first three columns in this table deal with the individuals who were playing each game in 1987 and describe what happened to their participation in the sport in question over the next 12 months. The final column deals with the sample members who were not playing the sports in 1987 (though most were playing other games) and gives the percentages who took up the activities during 1988. This evidence highlights the high level of mobility in sporting lives. Bowls had the most stable, and the oldest body of players, but even in this sport only 67 percent of the participants in 1987 continued to play at exactly the same rate in 1988. Among the other sports, snooker had the least stable players – only 34 percent of the 1987 participants maintained their previous rate of activity in 1988. Swimming, badminton, and keep-fit and weight training are the sports in Table 6.2 in which the proportions of 1987 players who increased and reduced their involvement during 1988 were similar and fairly high (between 25 and 30 percent in every case). Also, these sports had high rates of recruitment (13 to 30 percent) from respondents who were not playing the games in 1987. These are examples of sports in which many individuals with continuous careers were increasing or reducing their involvement depending partly on their other sport commitments, and which were often played as secondary rather than primary games.

Table 6.2 *Changes in participation in specific sports (1987-1988)*

	Off all who were playing in 1987: percentages who			Percentages of non-participants in 1987 who played the sports regularly in 1988
	a. Reduced	*b. Stayed the same*	*c. Increased participation*	
Snooker	38	34	28	8
Swimming	30	42	28	30
Martial Arts	29	56	15	4
Keep-fit/weights	26	47	27	25
Badminton	25	50	25	13
Soccer	24	59	18	8
Bowls	15	67	18	8

Snooker, martial arts and soccer had more 1987 participants who reduced than increased their involvement during 1988, and had relatively low rates of recruitment from non-players (no higher than eight percent). The apparent decline in the popularity of these sports will be partly due to the fact that they are all predominantly young people's games, and our sample was growing older throughout the research. However, it is also likely, particularly in the cases of snooker and the (mainly eastern) martial arts, that after a boom in the early-1980s these activities were suffering a decline in fashion. Keep-fit and weight training, in contrast, were vogue activities during the period of our research. This is why the local authorities were introducing more exercise classes and opening fitness suites, and why the commercial sector was offering comparable facilities.

Sport is susceptible to swings in fashion. Even sports that have been prominent for decades experience upswings and downturns in appeal. Minor sports flourish then wane almost to the point of extinction. This means that it would not be sensible for us to recommend specific sports as particularly suitable for attracting or retaining young or older players, or males or females. We can be confident that such recommendations drawn directly from our evidence would become outdated very rapidly. The implication of our evidence is that sport promotion needs to be flexible. High rates of drop-out from particular sports have to be accepted as inevitable given the fluidity of the typical sport career. Our advice to promoters is to tolerate drop-out, concentrate on recruitment, and be prepared to follow trends in fashion. In our view, there is no one best way in sport provision. Plural provisions – many types of centres under the different styles of management that characterise the public, voluntary and commercial sectors – will be the best guarantee of flexibility and responsiveness to demand.

7

THE COMPONENTS OF PERSONAL HEALTH AND FITNESS

The measurements

Our research was designed to explain levels and patterns of sport activity and, in particular, to establish the best types of provisions, and to whom they should be marketed, so as to make the strongest possible impact. A complementary and equally important objective was to measure the health and fitness benefits, if any, derived by the ordinary recreational players that we studied as opposed particularly to serious or professional athletes, and those willing to follow the fitness regimes prescribed in experimental studies. This second set of objectives made it desirable to study a large sample of male and female players aged from 16 into the retirement age groups. As explained previously, when initially contacted they were mostly playing one of seven selected sports, the exceptions being the smaller number of non-players who were recruited to the study in 1987. Some, but not all of the seven sports that the participants were playing when first contacted were competitive games, and some but not all were energetic activities. As described in previous chapters, the participants were playing at various frequencies from less than once a week to virtually every day and some had continuous whereas others had interrupted lifetime careers in sport. The size and composition of this sample allow us to explore the frequencies and regularity with which different types of sport needed to be played by different types of people in order for specific health and fitness effects to arise, and the research was given its longitudinal design primarily so as to investigate whether changes in levels and types of sport activity were accompanied by changes in health and fitness.

We have debated at length the contested meanings of health and fitness elsewhere (Lamb et al, 1988). Suffice it to say here, firstly, that we do not believe it useful to offer or seek precise and rigid definitions. Every investigation can be regarded as contributing to a better understanding of these states, but without reaching final answers. Secondly, however, along with most other recent researchers in the field, we have rejected the equation of good health with the mere absence of illness and impairment. Our evidence corroborates the view that there are different degrees of positive health. Whether it is useful to regard illness and positive health as situated at the poles of a continuum is, in our view, more debatable. The genetic and lifestyle factors that minimise the risks of illness may not, if present in stronger doses, push individuals up the positive planes of health. Correspondingly, activities which are particularly health-promoting may not reduce the risks of illness and injury. Health and fitness are complicated phenomena and our evidence suggests that they are better regarded as composed of many dimensions rather than unilinear scales. Thirdly, we initially adopted, and have retained the view that both negative and positive health and fitness have physical and socio-psychological components. Perfect health may be regarded as the maximisation of physical and socio-psychological well-being. Our measurements of health and fitness, therefore, included assessments of the subjects' attitudes and feelings about their condition. In our view, these measurements do not require validation against more objective physical indicators. "Feeling well" is not just a likely consequence of, but also part of what people are likely to mean by being healthy. Indeed, it can be argued that the simple question, "How well do you feel?" is as useful as any other single indicator of a person's overall state of health (MacIntyre, 1986). The health measurements employed in this research were chosen in order to explore the physical and socio-psychological dimensions, and simultaneously the negative and positive planes of health and fitness. However, we were also governed by the types and number of measurements to which respondents could reasonably be subjected at sports centres and in their homes.

Our initial confident expectation, based on previous research, was that, on at least some measurements, frequency of sport participation would be positively related to "good" health scores, but we were aware of the naivety of assuming that simple correlations would prove causation. Hence the longitudinal design of our research. Hence also the collection of information about many other aspects of the sample's circumstances and everyday lifestyles with a potential bearing on their health and fitness. We asked about the subjects' occupations, if any, incomes, types of housing and living conditions, diets, exercise apart from sport in everyday life, alcohol consumption and use of tobacco products. As a result, we can check whether any superior health among the more frequent sport participants could have been due to other health promoting features of their social situations or lifestyles. Also, in so far as sport participation was making an independent difference, we can compare its strength with other influences on the sample's personal health systems.

Altogether we measured 32 different indicators of the sample's health and fitness and, in addition, incorporated a stress questionnaire within the 1987 and 1988 home interviews. All these indicators are listed in Table 7.1. Seven verbal questions were included in the 1986 facility-based survey, and all of these items were repeated in the home interviews in 1987 and 1988. On each of these occasions we obtained the respondents' reported height and weight,

Table 7.1 *Health and Fitness Measurements*

1986	1987	1988
Questions		
1. Height	1. Height	1. Height
2. Weight	2. Weight	2. Weight
3. Self-assessed health	3. Self-assessed health	3. Self-assessed health
4. Self-assessed fitness	4. Self-assessed fitness	4. Self-assessed fitness
5. Doctors' visits	5. Doctors' visits	5. Doctors' visits
6. Medicines	6. Medicines	6. Medicines
7. Sleep	7. Sleep	7. Sleep
	8. Stress	8. Stress
Home tests		
	9. Screening questions	9. Screening questions
	10. Blood pressure*	10. Blood pressure*
	11. Pulse	11. Pulse
	12. Height	12. Height
	13. Weight	13. Weight
	14. Grip strength (both hands)	14. Grip strength(both hands)
	15. Lung function (FEV)	15. Lung function (FEV)
	16. Lung function (PEF)	16. Lung function (PEF)
	17. Lung function (FVC)	17. Lung function (FVC)
	18. Flexibility	18. Flexibility
		19. Abdominal circumference
		20. Hip circumference
Sports centre tests		
	21. Exclusion questions	21. Exclusion questions
	22. Aerobic capacity	22. Aerobic capacity
	23. Flexibility	23. Flexibility
	24. Leg power	24. Leg power
	25. Hand grip (both hands)	25. Hand grip (both hands)
	26. Height	26. Height
	27. Weight	27. Weight
	28. Waist measurement	28. Waist measurement
	29. Hip measurement	29. Hip measurement
	30. Skinfold thickness	30. Skinfold thickness
	31. Blood cholesterol	31. Blood cholesterol
	32. Blood pressure*	32. Blood pressure*
	33. Pulse	33. Pulse

*systolic and diastolic

and their self-assessed health and fitness (excellent, good, fair, poor or very poor) compared with other people of the same age. We also asked whether they had visited a doctor during the last six months, whether they were receiving medicines or other prescribed drugs regularly, and whether they considered that they normally slept very well, satisfactorily, poorly or very poorly. Stress was measured in the 1987 and 1988 home interviews through a battery of nine questions which asked about the subjects' ability to concentrate, whether they lost sleep through worry, broke into sweat without taking exercise, felt under strain, unable to overcome their difficulties, that things were getting on top of them, experienced tension at times in the neck, shoulders or head, felt their nerves jangling, and whether they considered themselves more or less stressed than other people. Responses to each of these questions were scored from 1 to 3 giving total stress scores with a range of 9 to 27. All nine variables used in constructing this scale were strongly correlated, so the scale had excellent construct validity within our sample. The mean score in 1987 was 14.9 and 15.0 in 1988.

Also, in the 1987 and 1988 home surveys the interviewers were especially trained and carried the equipment to conduct a set of simple tests which were administered to subjects who did not object (no-one did) and who survived the relevant screening questions asking, again, whether they were taking prescribed pills or medicines, recovering from a medical condition, surgery, injury or flu, suffered fainting spells or dizziness, or had any history of heart complaints, back pains, bronchitis, asthma, high or low blood pressure. In both 1987 and 1988 51 percent of the respondents "failed" one or more of these screening questions, though only 11 percent in 1987 and 3 percent in 1988 believed that any aspect of their condition prevented them from taking part in a full fitness assessment. Nevertheless, other subjects were excluded from certain tests. For example, those with any indications of heart, fainting or blood pressure problems were exempted from all the measurements except of height and weight. When there were no grounds for any exclusions, three measurements of blood pressure (systolic and diastolic) and pulse rate were also taken. Grip strength was measured with a hand dynamometer through two maximal trials with each hand. Each subject was given three tests of lung function using a portable digital spirometer in which measurements were taken of forced expired volume, peak expired flow, and forced vital capacity. Flexibility was tested with a sit and reach board which measured the distance that each subject could reach in relation to his or her feet. Also, in 1988 only, measurements of abdominal and hip circumference was taken. There were no "casualties" during these tests, nor any subsequent complaints about after-effects, or the procedures themselves. We had wondered whether non-specialist interviewers could be trained, and would be willing to take these measurements accurately, but in the event this was not a problem. Rather, we found that the fieldworkers were mostly delighted to be involved in a non-routine investigation. We also wondered whether the subjects would object to physical tests in their homes, but everyone's impression was that this aspect of the investigation increased the response to, and the acceptability of the research. Most subjects seemed far more interested in having their health and fitness assessed than in answering questions about their leisure.

Some of the home measurements were repeated with a sub-sample of 372 in 1987 and 244 in 1988 who accepted invitations to local sports centres for further tests. Individuals who attended were given similar screening questions to those used in their homes. Again, our initial fear that sample members would be unwilling to face additional tests proved unfounded: we faced the opposite problem of needing to ration this facility. With the centre-tested sub-sample we repeated the home measurements of flexibility, height, weight, waist, hips, blood pressure and pulse. This was primarily to check the accuracy of the home measurements, and in all cases the correspondences were high. In addition, the sub-sample members were given a test of aerobic capacity which was estimated from heart rate response to incremental sub-maximal cycle ergometry. Chest electrodes and a digital heart rate monitor were used, and initial workloads were related to the subjects' lean body masses. Leg power was assessed using a maximal vertical jump test in which a digital jump meter was attached at one end around the subject's waist. Skinfold thickness was measured with callipers, while blood cholesterol was measured from 32 microlitre samples by dry chemistry reflectance photo-metry.

For the purposes of analysis some of the above measurements were combined to produce composite indicators of health and fitness. The screen-ing questions were used in this way to create unhealthiness scales, height and weight were combined to yield body mass index scores, and likewise the abdominal and hip measurements.

Analysis

We have examined each health and fitness indicator separately and com-pared the sample's scores by sport participation, age, sex and socio-economic status in most possible combinations. Presenting all the evidence in full would be tortuous; unnecessarily so because eventually we found that reality was less complicated. Most of the measurements are best regarded not as discrete and independent variables but as alternative indicators of broader underlying health and fitness conditions.

We identified these underlying conditions through factor analysis, a well-established set of statistical procedures for condensing a larger set of measurements into a smaller number of variables. When all the measure-ments in such an analysis turn-out to be strongly related to each other, this suggests that they are all indicating a single underlying condition, which we would have described as health, had a single underlying factor been indi-cated, given the character of our measurements. Alternatively, if more than a single factor is identified, and we will show that this was the case with our measurements, the analysis is a way of establishing exactly what the separate underlying conditions are.

Some cautionary comments may be useful before presenting any results from the analysis. Firstly, like other research evidence the findings do not speak for themselves but require intelligent interpretation, in this instance in the light of what is independently known about personal health and fitness, and the measurements used in our study. Secondly, it is inevitably the case that the variables identified in factor analysis depend on the measurements that are initially fed in, and our fieldwork adopted merely a selection from a much larger number of possible health and fitness measurements. We were able to run separate factor analyses with the 1987 and 1988 findings, in each case firstly including only the verbal and physical home measurements, then with the smaller sub-samples for whom the results from the centre tests were also available. Predictably, these several analyses did not yield completely identical results which made it necessary to select the best overall solution, namely, the factors identified in all the computations from both years' results.

In all the analyses four main health and fitness factors were identified repeatedly. The factor that accounted for more variance than any other across all the measurements in the model can be described as *strength*, and was best indicated by the various assessments of lung function and grip. The second factor, which we name *cardiovascular*, was identified primarily by the various blood pressure and pulse measurements. The sample's body mass scores also loaded on this factor, though not as heavily as the blood pressure and pulse readings, and likewise the sample's waist:hip ratios and flexibility scores. The third factor was identified through the health and fitness *self-assessments*, while the fourth, which we call *illness-free*, was identified by the screening items for the physical tests, plus the questions on doctor visits, and use of medicines and other prescribed drugs. Table 7.2 describes how the critical measurements in the 1988 home tests and interviews loaded onto these four factors.

It will be immediately apparent that these health and fitness factors do not divide neatly into one set which can be meaningfully described as health, and another as fitness. Our respondents themselves seemed to experience little difficulty in distinguishing between their fitness and health. Very few appeared confused when asked to rate themselves separately using these twin yardsticks. Some who regarded their health as excellent did not rate themselves as fully fit. When they described themselves as healthy most individuals seemed to mean that their lives were normally unimpaired by illness or disability. When they described themselves as fit they seemed to mean that they were tuned-up to maximum performance. Our illness-free component probably corresponds most closely with what the subjects themselves meant by being healthy, but the other components do not dovetail neatly with their everyday meanings of fitness. The strength and cardiovascular factors, and the self-assessments, contain elements of the everyday meanings of both fitness and health. In terms of how their systems actually functioned as opposed to in our subjects' minds, health and fitness were not clearly distinguishable components. Subsequently, therefore, we will refer to all the factors simply as health components.

It will also be immediately apparent that many of our 32 measurements were not encompassed by any of the four factors, but this does not automatically invalidate them as health indicators. Some indicators may have been isolated by our failure to take other measurements which would then have

Table 7.2   *Factor Analysis, 1988 Home Interviews and Tests
(selected variables)*

Variable	Communality	Factor	Eigenvalue	% of Var.	Cum.%
Body mass index	.31538	1	3.44565	26.5	26.5
Flexibility	.22672	2	1.87367	14.4	40.9
Waist: Hips	.31127	3	1.54147	11.9	52.8
Systolic blood pressure	.71532	4	1.22542	9.4	62.2
Diastolic blood pressure	.68678				
Grip	.75337				
Forced expired volume	.87228				
Forced vital capacity	.80209				
Peak expired flow	.66251				
Self-assessed fitness	.79526				
Doctor visits	.61468				
Self-assessed health	.73013				
Medicines	.60041				

Varimax rotated factor matrix

	Factor 1	Factor 2	Factor 3	Factor 4
Body mass index	.09986	.54660	-.05066	.06378
Flexibility	.14286	-.38400	.19579	.14326
Waist: Hips	.34211	.41056	-.16000	.00832
Systolic blood pressure	.27318	.78938	.12475	.04483
Diastolic blood pressure	-.05943	.82521	.04410	.01794
Grip	.82547	.26692	.02685	.00147
Forced expired volume	.93293	-.04307	.00707	.00423
Forced vital capacity	.89518	-.01591	-.01242	-.01840
Peak expired flow	.80671	.09455	.05276	-.00290
Self-assessed fitness	.07563	-.09911	.88283	.01801
Doctor visits	-.01563	-.04667	-.02841	.78195
Self-assessed health	-.06125	.01149	.84786	-.08592
Medicines	-.00824	.07846	-.05211	.77043

allowed additional factors to be identified. Furthermore, particular measurements could have been susceptible to a number of underlying conditions. Sleep difficulties, for example, could have been due to any number of physical and psychological problems, which is probably why this particular item did not load heavily onto any single health factor. The stress scale did not load consistently onto any of the four health factors identified, and is therefore treated as an additional independent indicator throughout the following discussion.

For each of the other four factors that the analysis identified, two factor scores were calculated for each respondent based on the questions and tests administered in the subjects' homes in 1987 and 1988 respectively. In each case the scales were transformed to make all the scores positive, that is, above zero, and so that the higher the reading the better the individual's health. However, we have not inverted the stress scale. In this instance, therefore, the least stressed individuals have the lowest scores, whereas those with low blood pressure and pulse readings have high scores on the cardio-vascular health factor. We must emphasise that individuals' factor scores are only meaningful in relation to other individuals' scores on the same factors and within each year. Taken separately and in isolation the scores are meaningless. Moreover, the strength and cardiovascular scores, for example, cannot be compared to conclude that the sample was healthier in terms of one factor than the other. However, the scores are powerful tools for com-paring the strength, cardiovascular conditions, self-assessments, freedom from illness and stress levels of various sub-groups of respondents.

According to our measurements, the male sample members were gen-erally the stronger, the females had the better cardiovascular scores overall, but there was little difference between the sexes' illness scores or self-assess-ments. With increasing age there was a deterioration in strength and cardio-vascular scores, little change in illness, and an improvement in self-assess-ments which is a normal finding when samples are asked to rate their own health and fitness relative to other people of the same age. Overall, socio-economic status was related to favourable scores on all the health factors which, once again, merely reflects a well-known relationship, this time between social class and health throughout the UK population. Stress scores, however, were not related to a statistically significant extent within our sample to either sex, age or socio-economic status. Our main interest, need-less to say, was in the differences, if any, that various types and levels of sport activity were making to the health factor and stress scores.

Our evidence points firmly to the conclusion that sport was making a positive difference, but before presenting the relevant findings and develop-ing this argument a further note of caution is needed. It would be unsafe to assume, and we do not believe, that all our findings and conclusions would hold in a random sample of the entire UK population. To begin with, there is no guarantee even that identical health factors would be distinguished. It certainly cannot be assumed that the importance of sport in governing our sample's health would apply throughout the wider population. Our sample was loaded with frequent players. Sport is certain to be less influential in accounting for variations in health within sections of the public with lower rates of activity. The sample selection in our study was deliberately biased so as to highlight sport effects. Rather than portraying the current contribution of sport to the general public's health, our findings and conclusions relate to sport's likely contribution if nationwide participation ever reached the norms for our atypically active sample.

8

LEVELS OF SPORT PARTICIPATION AND LEVELS OF HEALTH

Our main findings on the relationships between sport participation and health can be stated simply and precisely. The more frequently they played energetic sport, the better were individuals' self-assessment and strength scores, whereas there were no statistically significant relationships, positive or negative, with the cardiovascular or illness-free scores. These findings held throughout the sample as whole and within all sub-groups defined by age, sex and socio-economic status. Which particular sports were played seemed to make no difference, provided the games were energetic. Frequency and continuity of activity were the features of energetic sport participation with health effects. The sole inconsistency in our evidence is that the expected health trends according to changes in sport activity between 1987 and 1988 failed to appear.

There was also a major exception in our evidence that sport participation needed to be energetic to confer health benefits. This concerned the sample's stress scores. These were not related to a statistically significant extent to their levels of either energetic or non-energetic sport participation. However, high total sport participation was related to reduced stress. A combination of energetic and non-energetic activity seemed to be the only sport recipe capable of reducing stress. This was the only health variable on which there appeared to be any interactive effects from particular combinations of different types of sport. Stress was also related to other lifestyles variables rather differently than all the other health factors, and so the determinants of stress are discussed separately and fully later on in chapter ten.

Levels of participation

Figures 8.1 and 8.2 respectively plot the 1987 and 1988 mean health factor and stress scores according to the sample's participation in energetic sports. In previous chapters we described how respondents were given participation scores according to the number of sports that they played and the frequency. The energetic scores now being considered were calculated by counting

Figure 8.1

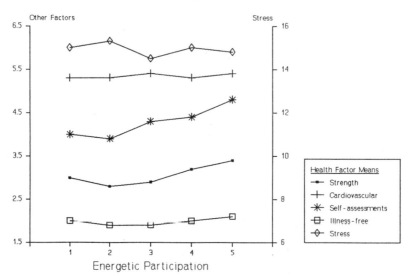

participation only in strenuous sports, so darts, snooker, cards, bowls, and so on were excluded.

Five participation levels are recognised in Figures 8.1 and 8.2. The least active group was not playing any energetic sport at all while the top group was participating more than five times per week.

It can be seen in both sets of graphs that as levels of energetic sport activity rose, so did the respondents' mean self-assessments and strength scores. Self-assessments rose progressively with each step up the sport participation scale, whereas strength scores exhibited a clear upward thrust only in the two top participation groups where individuals were playing at least three times a week. This suggests that sport activity needed to be not only energetic but also quite frequent, at least every other day, if individuals were to reap significant strength benefits.

These findings were replicated when the sample was sub-divided by sex, age and socio-economic status. All sections of the population seemed to be deriving the same kinds and levels of health benefit from participant sport. This evidence is cross-sectional and in itself does not prove that sport was the causal factor, though such an interpretation is consistent with everything that is known about exercise physiology and the results of experimental studies. In so far as sport was yielding health benefits, our findings suggest

Figure 8.2

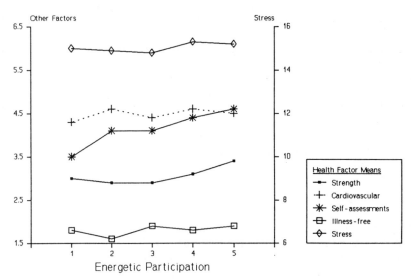

that these were operating mainly through the participants' self-assessments and strength, specifically in the case of the strength factor through their lung function and muscular power.

The absence of a clear relationship between energetic sport activity and cardiovascular scores may seem surprising. Some of the health benefits hitherto claimed for sport are supposed to arise through exercising and thereby strengthening the heart. Actually the sample's raw scores on some of the measurements that loaded onto the cardiovascular factor (blood pressure, pulse, and body mass scores) were related to sport activity, though only weakly, and not consistently within all socio-demographic groups. We did *not* find that these indicators were completely unrelated to sport participation. However, the cardiovascular improvements linked to sport activity were little greater than would normally have been expected to accompany gains in strength. We will explain later that the sample's cardiovascular scores were more strongly and directly governed by other lifestyle and socio-demographic variables.

The above caveats apply also to the absence of a clear relationship between the sample's sport activity and illness-free scores. There were some weak relationships in the raw data, but once again, not consistently within all socio-demographic groups. The crucial fact of the situation seemed to be that sport activity was not among the more powerful determinants of the sample's vulnerability to colds, flu and other ailments, accidents and injuries. In some ways the absence of a negative relationship between sport participation and freedom from illnesses is noteworthy because sport itself had been a quite common source of injuries. Nineteen percent of the respondents in the 1986 facility survey reported having suffered at least one sport injury at some time or another. The incidence of injuries varied considerably according to the sports that the individuals were playing when surveyed. Injuries had been most common among those practising martial arts (38 percent), badminton (27 percent) and soccer (24 percent). In contrast, only three percent of the bowls players reported injuries. Some of the injuries had been far from trivial. Forty-seven percent of those injured had been prevented from playing their sports temporarily, and in 46 percent of these cases the injuries had lasted for at least a month. The fact that the most frequent players in our sample did not have the poorest illness-free scores could be regarded as evidence that sport must have been conferring some compensating benefits.

Types of sport

All respondents were given non-energetic sport participation scores calculated in exactly the same way as their energetic scores, and these scores were used to examine whether any health factors varied systematically according to how often individuals played bowls, snooker and other non-strenuous games. The outcome of this analysis can be summarised very briefly; there were no relationships whatsoever that survived the introduction of controls for sex and age. There were no signs of the participants' health actually suffering from devotion to non-strenuous pastimes, but for sport to be beneficial it was clear that the activities needed to be energetic.

We also investigated whether some energetic sports were more health promoting than others. For this purpose we did not categorise individuals as soccer players and so on depending on the sports that they were playing when first contacted. As explained earlier, most sample members were active in several sports. In examining the health effects of specific sports, therefore, we considered separately the groups who, in 1987, were involved in martial arts at least once a week, then similarly defined groups for soccer, badminton, swimming and so on. Some individuals featured in more than one group. This was unavoidable. The vast majority of the regular participants in all the sports were also playing other games; there were too few singletons in our sample to retain worthwhile numbers while controlling for age, sex and levels of participation simultaneously. The procedure adopted was not statistically ideal, but it was the best available for investigating if regular participation in some of the sports for which we had adequate numbers of players was proving more beneficial for health than others.

Some of the sport groups initially appeared outstandingly healthy. For example, the soccer players were on average by far the strongest sample members, but this turned out to be entirely explicable in terms of the virtually all-male composition of this sport group. Among the females the martial arts group had the best mean cardiovascular scores, but this was entirely due to the participants' concentration in the youngest age group. With the previously noted exception of stress scores, the particular sports, or mixtures of sports, that individuals played did not appear to be governing the health benefits, provided the games were energetic. Neither competitive nor non-competitive activities were clearly superior. It was frequency, the number of occasions on which individuals played per week, that was making the difference. Our evidence corroborates an assumption in an earlier analysis of General Household Survey data by Gratton and Tice (1989) that on average participants adjust the length and intensity of their play so as to roughly equalise the exercise value of each separate occasion when any energetic sport is played.

Figure 8.3

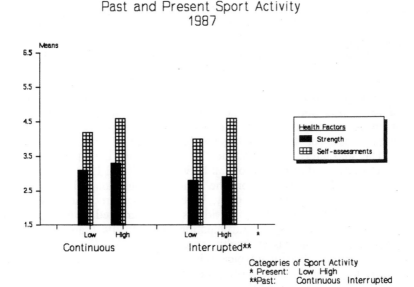

Health and
Past and Present Sport Activity
1987

Categories of Sport Activity
* Present: Low High
**Past: Continuous Interrupted

Trends over time

We were interested in the longitudinal relationships between health and sport participation within our sample for two reasons: firstly to examine whether any health effects were enduring after participation ceased or declined, and secondly to check the relationships demonstrated cross-sectionally. We investigated the relationships between the sample's health factor and stress scores, and their past and current levels of sport activity, by dividing the respondents into four groups according to whether their sport careers had been continuous or interrupted, then by whether their energetic participation in 1987 was high or low relative to the sample norm. We explained in chapter three that individuals with continuous careers tended to be the most frequent current players, but there were enough exceptions to permit the analysis now being described. Figure 8.3 plots the mean scores for each group's two principal health factors that were most sensitive to energetic sport activity, namely, self-assessments and strength. Two conclusions can be drawn. Firstly, with past participation held constant, current levels of activity were positively related to the sample's current strength and self-assessment scores. The clear message here is that sport participation needed to be sustained if individuals were to retain the full benefits (see also Morris et al, 1990). Secondly, with current participation levels held constant, continuous participation in the past was related to higher current strength, but not self-assessment scores than would otherwise have been expected. Self-assessments appeared to be more sensitive, indeed exclusively sensitive, to current participation, but this did not apply to strength. This latter health benefit from sport appeared to be enduring, albeit in a diluted form, even if individuals subsequently reduced their participation. However, it must be borne in mind that the individuals who were retaining this benefit had not abandoned sport completely.

All the above findings, about the need for participation to persist in order to achieve the full potential benefits, and the extinction of self-assessment benefits once participation ended or declined as opposed to the more enduring character of the strength gains, held within all socio-demographic groups. The sole internal inconsistency in our evidence is that the sample's health factor scores did not rise or fall between 1987 and 1988 in the directions that would be predicted from the above findings alongside changes in their levels of energetic sport activity. When we compared the changes in strength and self-assessments of individuals who increased with those who reduced their energetic sport participation between 1987 and 1988, the changes in the sport increasers' health scores were not significantly different from the decreasers'. The ideal typical scientist is supposed to strive to refute hypotheses, but probably like most practising investigators, we hunted for longitudinal evidence to corroborate the cross-sectional relationships that we had discovered. We sub-divided the sport increasers and decreasers in several ways in our efforts to make the expected health changes appear. For example, we restricted the comparisons to just those who had increased or decreased substantially rather than marginally, and we separated those who had changed from high and low starting points. Despite these endeavours, the expected relationships just would not emerge from the data.

No-one can ever prove conclusively why a relationship does not exist, but our two best guesses are, firstly, that all other relevant things had not remained constant. Overall our evidence gives qualified support to the health-promoting case for energetic sport. The effects apparent in our evidence were beneficial overall despite the prevalence of sport injuries. However, sport participation was not operating directly upon all the principal health factors that our analysis identified, and the next chapter explains that other lifestyle and socio-economic influences were exerting more pervasive and often stronger effects on the sample's health and fitness. We suspect that the effects of changes in our respondents' sport activity between 1987 and 1988 had been over-ridden by these other influences. Our second best guess is that changes in levels of sport activity were not having powerful and immediate effects on both of the health factors that were cross-sectionally related to participation. If strength effects were enduring, as suggested earlier, individuals' scores were unlikely to fall and rise immediately alongside changes in their levels of sport activity. Sport could not realistically aspire to win both ways on this matter. Participants could not reasonably expect immediate strength benefits from increasing their activity, and that some of these gains would survive even if they did not sustain their new levels of participation.

9

OTHER LIFESTYLE INFLUENCES UPON
HEALTH AND FITNESS

Other lifestyle variables

Our research was meant to go beyond rediscovering that sport participants are mostly healthier and fitter than the population in general. As previous chapters have demonstrated, we wanted to identify the main ports of entry through which sport participation was affecting personal health systems, together with the types of sports, and the frequency and persistence of participation required to obtain specified benefits. Also, throughout the analysis and presentation of the findings, we have taken care to ensure that any superior health recorded by the sport participants could not have been merely a reflection of their tending to be male, young and middle class. The sport effects identified above were apparent within all socio-demographic groups.

We were also aware that respondents' health was likely to depend upon many lifestyle practices apart from sport participation. So any superior health of the participants might have been due to other health promoting features of their lifestyles or socio-economic circumstances. Hence the design of the research to test whether sport was making an independent and possibly unique contribution to the participants' personal health and fitness. We wanted to assess the importance of sport relative to other influences on the participants' health. Accordingly the 1987 and 1988 home interviews included detailed questions about selected aspects of the sample's everyday lifestyles; range and frequency of overall leisure activity, exercise apart from sport, diet, tobacco use and alcohol consumption. The findings presented below are mostly from the 1987 survey, but all the statistically significant relationships highlighted in our interpretations were also present in 1988.

Other exercise
For the purposes of analysis we have divided the sample into three groups according to whether their self-reported "other exercise" was low, moderate or high, and Figure 9.1 shows how their health factor and stress scores varied. The apparent health effects of "other exercise" were very similar to

Figure 9.1

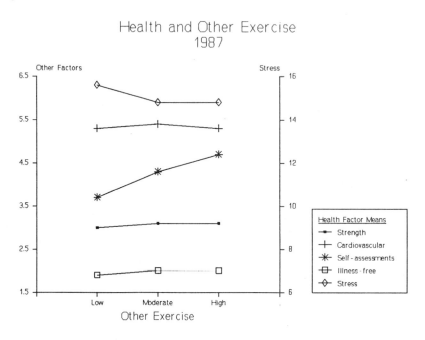

sport, which is hardly surprising, but with one interesting exception. There were no significant relationships with the cardiovascular, illness-free or strength factor scores. The latter relationship ran in the predicted direction but was not statistically significant which is consistent with our earlier observation that to obtain significant strength benefits exercise needed to be frequent and vigorous. So a non-sedentary job, walking the dog and suchlike were not conferring measurable strength benefits. In contrast, exercise in everyday life was strongly related to the sample's self-assessments. It was also related to low stress scores. This was among the few statistically significant relationships that we were able to identify between stress and other variables. Gentler exercise seemed to be more stress reducing than high rates of participation in energetic sport. It is worth recalling from Figures 8.1 and 8.2 that stress scores dipped (though not to a statistically significant extent) among respondents with "moderate" rates of energetic sport participation, just two or three times a week.

The sample's overall patterns and levels of leisure activity are discussed fully in chapter ten. However, we can note here that these general levels and patterns bore no relationships whatsoever to scores on the strength, cardio-vascular, self-assessment or illness-free factors.

Figure 9.2

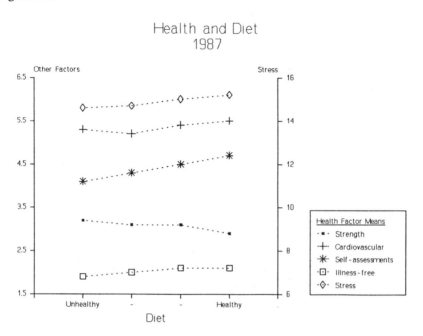

Diet

Respondents were asked about their consumption of various foodstuffs and their diets were rated as healthy if they were relatively free of sugar, fatty foods, red and processed meat, and rich in fresh fruit, vegetables, fish, poultry and high fibre substances. The sample was then split into four groups according to the overall healthiness of their diets, and these groups' mean health factor and stress scores are presented in Figure 9.2. No positive effects of diet upon strength were evident. Indeed, respondents with the least healthy diets turned out to be the strongest on average. They also had the lowest stress scores. It is unlikely that otherwise health promoting diets could have been actually increasing stress, but it is entirely plausible that high stress was one of the circumstances prompting the individuals concerned to diet carefully.

Chapter ten explains that high levels of stress were related to individuals changing not only their diets but also other aspects of their lifestyles with the intention of improving their well-being, but certainly as far as stress levels were concerned, most of these intended health steps were not related to any measurable improvement. However, our evidence suggests that individuals with sensible diets were deriving other health benefits because good scores

Figure 9.3

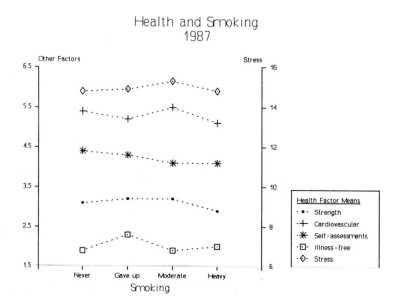

Figure 9.4

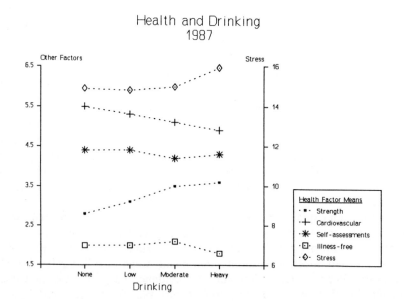

on our diet scale were related to good health on the cardiovascular, self-assessment, and illness-free factors.

Tobacco
The sample was divided into heavy and moderate smokers, while abstainers were divided into those who had never smoked and those who had given up. According to the findings in Figure 9.3, tobacco use was not affecting the sample's illness or stress scores, but it was related to poor health on all the other indicators, namely the strength, cardiovascular and self-assessment factors.

Alcohol
Nil or moderate alcohol consumption appeared to be beneficial in terms of staying illness-free and enjoying good cardiovascular health. Heavy drinking was related to high stress scores, though this relationship was not statistically significant, and alcohol consumption was the only lifestyle factor in our entire analysis which, while associated with other health benefits, was completely unrelated to the sample's self-assessments. Also, the heaviest drinkers turned out to be the strongest sample members (see Figure 9.4), but this relationship was not an alcohol effect. Like the relationship between poor dieting and strength, it was entirely due to the heaviest drinkers tending to be young males. The higher susceptibility of the heavy drinkers to poor cardiovascular health and illnesses is hardly surprising, but the absence of any relationship with the sample's self-assessments deserves comment.

Whether a lifestyle practice affects the actors' self-assessed health and fitness is likely to depend on whether they believe that the activity is damaging or beneficial. Evidence from this research presented in earlier chapters shows that most respondents believed that exercise, including sport, was generally good for their health and fitness. The majority seemed to accept that tobacco use was damaging, and that their food intake could have health implications. In contrast, the sample appeared far more resistant to anti-alcohol health propaganda.

Relative contributions

It could be counter-productive, scientifically and socially, even to pose the question of whether sport was more or less health promoting than other lifestyle variables. The answer would inevitably depend upon "how much" of each was involved. In any case, our evidence shows that different practices were operating upon different components in individuals' personal health systems, so the effects were not directly comparable. Every lifestyle variable that we measured, except alcohol consumption, was related to self-assessments. Healthy diets and low or nil alcohol consumption seemed the best recipe for staying illness-free. These same lifestyle variables, plus not smoking, made the best combination for impacting directly and positively on

Figure 9.5

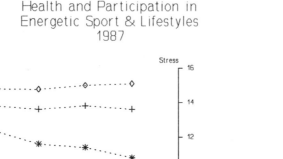

Health and Participation in
Energetic Sport & Lifestyles
1987

Sport & Lifestyle *

* Sport & Lifestyle Participation Groups
1= High & Healthy   2= High & Unhealthy
3= Low & Healthy   4= Low & Unhealthy

cardiovascular health. Playing sport and not smoking seemed the best combination for increasing strength. Other exercise, plus high overall participation in energetic and non-energetic sport, and unhealthy diets, were the lifestyle practices associated with low stress scores, though probably not causally in the latter case.

Figure 9.5 divides the sample into four groups, firstly according to whether their energetic sport participation was above or below average, then by whether they scored above or below average for the sample on a lifestyle index based on their smoking, eating and drinking habits, and exercise apart from sport. These diagrams present the mean scores for the four groups thus defined on the principal health factors. It can be seen that with other lifestyle factors held constant, high levels of energetic sport activity were improving the individuals' strength and self-assessments, while with levels of energetic sport activity controlled, individuals who were above-average in other healthy practices had the better scores on the illness-free and cardiovascular scales and, again, on the self-assessment factor. The contributions to health and fitness of the different lifestyle practices were clearly additive. However healthily they lived in other respects, individuals could expect further benefits by playing sport, abstaining from alcohol and tobacco, and sensible eating. None of these practices made the others superfluous. Nor did any immunise the actors against the risk of damage normally associated with unhealthy lifestyles. Some sport players, mostly young males, expressed the belief, or hope, that their exercise freed them from worry about their eating and drinking on other occasions. Indeed, it was not unusual for sport and drinking to be parts of the same days or evenings out. No-one expressed the view that their attention to diet made regular exercise unnecessary, but such an argument would have been as specious as the young sportsmen's claim.

The preceding chapter explained that it was impossible to identify any links between changes in our sample's health, and changes in their sport behaviour between 1987 and 1988. One of our best guesses to explain the absence of such relationships was that other things that could have affected the sample's health, including the additional lifestyle variables subsequently considered, had not remained equal. Our other best guess was that the respondents' health was not improving or deteriorating rapidly alongside ups and downs in their sport activity, and this could also have applied to other lifestyle practices. It is likely that achieving the benefits depended on sustaining health promoting behaviour over an extended period. The corollary of this second hypothesis is that gains that had been gradually built-up were then likely to survive minor lifestyle fluctuations. The plausibility of this hypothesis is strengthened by an examination of the relationships, or rather their absence in most cases, between changes in the sample's health factor and stress scores between 1987 and 1988 and parallel trends in all the types of behaviour which this chapter has shown to be health relevant. On the basis of evidence collected in the 1988 home interviews we constructed a scale based on how many lifestyle changes involving sport, other exercise, diet, smoking, drinking, relaxing and reducing stress the individuals had made in the prior year to try to improve or maintain their health. The sample was then divided according to whether they had made none, just one, or more of these changes. As the number of health-promoting steps increased, self-assessments were more likely to have been preserved or to have improved, and this was the sole health factor that, within our sample, was responding immediately, to a statistically significant extent, to changes in sport activity and other lifestyle variables. On the other three health factors and on the stress scale the differences between the groups were not statistically significant.

Our evidence suggests, therefore, that if individuals wish to improve their health by adopting appropriate lifestyles they should be prepared to wait for at least a year to derive most of the ultimately measurable gains except in their self-assessments, then maintain their health promoting life patterns. The main short-term effect of favourable lifestyle changes, including increased sport participation, had been to leave the individuals concerned feeling healthier and fitter without any corresponding changes in their physical functioning.

Figure 9.6a

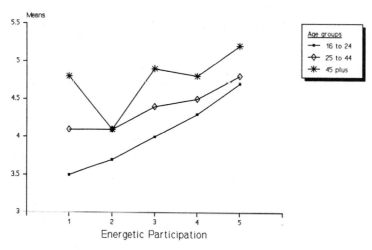

Figure 9.6b

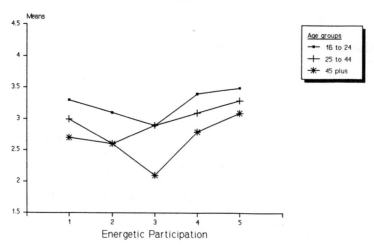

Socio-demographic statuses

Lifestyles are generally thought to be within individuals' own control. Sociologists may argue that some groups have more scope for choice than others and that everyone's choices are governed by prior socialisation, but no-one disputes that people have greater control over whether they smoke, how much they drink, what they eat, and whether to play sport than their age and sex, though gender and age roles may be susceptible to some social negotiation. Chapter seven described the main age and sex health inequalities within our sample. The males were the stronger while the females tended to have superior cardiovascular scores. Strength and cardiovascular scores declined with age while self-assessments improved, and whatever lifestyles they had adopted our respondents were proving no more able to avoid these normal health consequences than to actually change their ages or sex.

Lifestyle practices were definitely not obliterating age or sex inequalities. In the case of sport this can be seen clearly in Figures 9.6 and 9.7. High levels of sport activity were giving adults the strength of non-players 10 to 15 years younger, and the self-assessments of non-players 10 to 20 years older. However, at all levels of sport participation, strength declined and self-assessments improved with age, and even non-participant males had generally superior strength to the most sports-active females. At low levels of sport activity, men's self-assessments were slightly superior to women's overall, whereas at the higher participation levels the women had the best assessments. Women's feelings about their personal health and fitness seemed especially responsive to sport activity. However, sex differences in self-assessments were narrow at all levels of sport participation.

Socio-economic status stands midway between age and sex on the one hand, and lifestyles on the other, in terms of individuals' ability to take charge. People can change their socio-economic circumstances, but no amount of striving can alter the fact that there is only limited room at the top. Whereas it is at least conceivable that everyone might play sport and give up smoking, there is simply no way in which the entire population could obtain the best jobs and homes, and above-average incomes. However, these inequalities can be widened or narrowed by government policies, and it has been argued that the most effective way, possibly the only effective way, of improving the notoriously poor relative health of lower socio-economic groups will be to reduce their economic deprivations (Townsend, et al, 1988). A contrary argument is that the lower socio-economic groups would not endure poorer health if only they adopted sensible lifestyles. Our evidence offers more support for the former than the latter viewpoint.

To explore the interaction between socio-economic status, lifestyles and health we constructed two indices. Firstly, an index of socio-economic status was based on individuals' education, housing, normal occupations, and labour market experiences between 1986 and 1988. Socio-economic status, measured with this index, was strongly related to the sample's scores on every health

Figure 9.7a

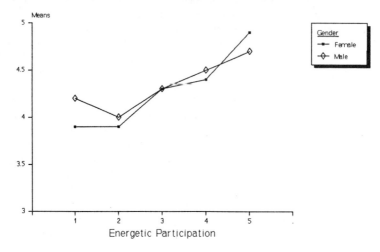

Self-Assessments and
Energetic Participation by Gender
1987

Figure 9.7b

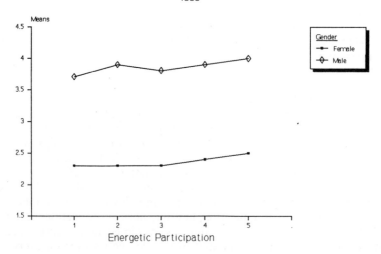

Strength and Energetic Participation
by Gender
1988

factor except stress (see Figure 9.8). It is perhaps noteworthy, firstly, that no other variable had such clear and pervasive health effects, and secondly that the variations by socio-economic status were especially wide on the same health factors as sport, namely strength and self-assessments. We also constructed a composite lifestyle index based on the sample's energetic sport participation, other exercise, alcohol use, diet, and use or non-use of tobacco products.

Figure 9.9 divides the sample into healthy, intermediate and unhealthy lifestyle groups according to their overall scores on this index, and simultaneously into those with relatively high and low socio-economic status. It can be seen that health promoting lifestyles were not usually over-riding the normal health effects of socio-economic status. With lifestyles controlled, socio-economic status remains positively related to health in eight out of the twelve relevant comparisons in Figure 9.9. Meanwhile, with socio-economic status held constant, there are linear relationships between lifestyles and health on just three out of the eight possible occasions.

Figure 9.8

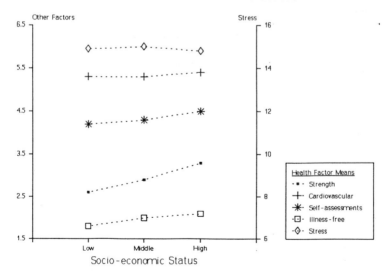

Health and Socio-economic Status

Figure 9.9a

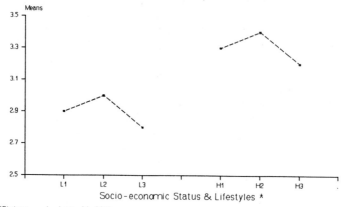

*Status: L= Low   H= High
Lifestyles:
1=Unhealthy   2=Intermediate   3=Healthy

Figure 9.9b

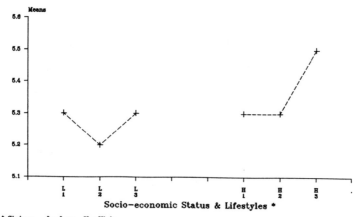

* Status: L= Low   H= High
Lifestyles:
1=Unhealthy   2=Intermediate   3=Healthy

The self-assessments of both the high and low socio-economic groups improved as their lifestyles became healthier, as did cardiovascular, illness-free and stress scores, though in the latter three cases only within the higher status group, which supports Blaxter's (1990) conclusions from the nation-wide (in Britain) Health and Lifestyle Survey. Firstly, within our sample socio-economic status was clearly playing a pivotal role in fixing health status because its effects were pervasive, operating on many of the health factors, and resilient, appearing within all age, sex and lifestyle groups. Secondly, the behaviour on which our study focused, sport participation, was not only most likely to be adopted by, but also, in concert with other everyday lifestyle practices, was tending to make the greatest difference to the health of the socio-economic groups that were health privileged to begin with.

This evidence qualifies without undermining the health promoting case for sport. It suggests that sport is useful alongside, but not as a substitute for other healthy lifestyle practices. Our evidence also suggests that promoting healthy lifestyles really can make a difference to the public's health, but that such measures of themselves will not eradicate or necessarily even lessen the inequalities associated with socio-economic status.

Figure 9.9c

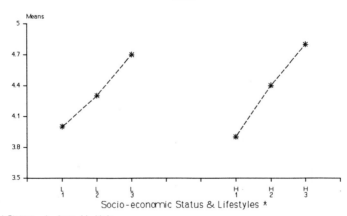

Self-assessments and
Socio-economic Status & Lifestyles
1987

* Status: L= Low   H= High
Lifestyles:
1=Unhealthy 2=Intermediate 3=Healthy

Figure 9.9d

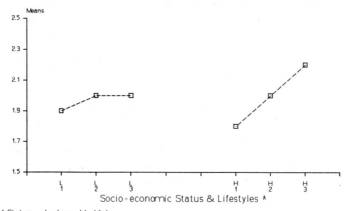

Illness-free and
Socio-economic Status & Lifestyles
1987

* Status: L= Low   H= High
Lifestyles:
1=Unhealthy 2=Intermediate 3=Healthy

Figure 9.9e

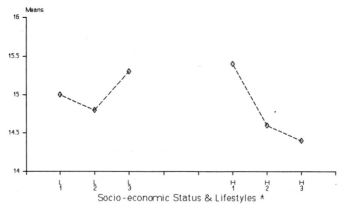

Stress and
Socio-economic Status & Lifestyles
1987

* Status: L= Low   H= High
Lifestyles:
1=Unhealthy 2=Intermediate 3=Healthy

10

HEALTH AND FITNESS CONSCIOUSNESS, SPORT AND THE REST OF LEISURE

There was a tendency for the same individuals to be involved in all the lifestyle practices that the previous chapter has shown to be health-promoting. So those who were playing the most sport were more likely than other individuals to be taking further exercise in their everyday lives, modifying their diets to improve their health, drinking moderately rather than heavily, and to have either given-up tobacco or never to have smoked. One reason why all these types of behaviour tended to co-exist was that the individuals concerned possessed a stronger than average health and fitness consciousness which was leading them to do a variety of health-seeking things. Their sport participation, dieting, moderate use of alcohol and avoidance of tobacco were all partly due to the importance that the individuals attached to keeping themselves fit and healthy. However, it would be misleading to describe their entire lifestyles as health promoting. For the majority, health and fitness were not even their main leisure objectives let alone life goals. Sport and other health promoting practices were merely elements in their rich and diverse leisure lives.

Health and fitness consciousness

We developed a scale measuring health and fitness consciousness (HFC) following the 1987 home interviews in which answers to six different attitude questions proved strongly related. Three of these questions related to fitness, two were about health, and the third was about diet. Respondents were asked which steps, from a list of nine possibilities ranging from relaxing to taking more exercise, and from altering their living arrangements to improving their sleeping habits, they thought that people could take to enhance their fitness. Answers to this question were scored according to the number of possibilities that individuals selected. The second fitness question concerned the levels of control that respondents felt they had over their own fitness. Possible answers here ranged from complete control to none at all. The two health questions were similar to these fitness items: how many steps individuals could take to improve, and how much control they believed they had over their health. As might have been expected, fewer people believed that they had complete control over their health (eight percent) than over their fitness (24 percent). Also, fewer people felt that exercise was good for their health than for their fitness, though the majority felt that both kinds of benefit followed (75 percent and 90 percent). The additional fitness question was about the importance that respondents attached to being fit, and the final question concerned the effects of diet on health and fitness. Answers to each of these questions were rated from 0 to 6 and added together to give HFC scores on a 36 point scale. The sample mean was 21.9, the highest score was 32 (one person only), and the lowest score was seven (again only one person). This HFC scale exhibited excellent construct validity within our sample. The variables used were all highly correlated: the probability of obtaining the correlations by chance was less than one in a thousand in most cases. The results were examined further using factor analysis to see whether this technique would separate the health variables from the fitness items but this was not the case. After varimax rotation of the results three factors emerged on which health and fitness loaded equally. These factors can be described as:

i.   A *limits of control* factor, representing how much control individuals felt they had over their health and fitness.
ii. An *elements of control* factor, representing the number of steps that individuals believed they could take to improve their fitness and health.
iii. The *importance of fitness* to the individual, and of diet for health and fitness.

Scores for each of these factors correlated positively, indicating that HFC was a consistent and well-defined value orientation within our sample.

Health promotion in everyday life

Respondents who played any sport had higher mean HFC scores than non-participants (22.2 compared with 20.3 in 1987). The sport players had the higher mean scores overall, and the more frequently they played the higher their scores tended to be. These scores rose step by step with frequency of sport participation (see Figure 10.1). High levels of sport activity, therefore, were associated with a strong health and fitness consciousness, meaning that the individuals placed exceptional value on keeping themselves fit and healthy, and believed that how they lived from day to day could affect these aspects of their well-being.

High HFC was related not only to high levels of sport activity, but also to engaging in additional kinds of health and fitness seeking behaviour that were reported in the 1987 interviews (Roberts, Asturias et al, 1990). It was related to:

Figure 10.1

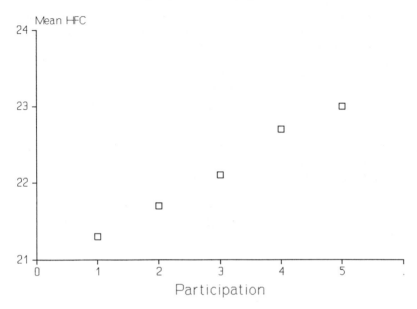

HFC by Sport Participation Level

i.   Taking plenty of exercise apart from sport in non-working life.
ii. Healthy diets as defined in the previous chapter, that is, relatively free
     of sugar, fatty foods, and red and processed meat, but rich in fresh
     fruit, vegetables, fish, poultry, and high fibre substances.
iii. Having made lifestyle changes during the previous 12 months such as
     taking more exercise, modifying diet, and trying to relax more and
     reduce stress, with the aim of achieving better health and fitness.
iv. In terms of use of tobacco products, the highest HFC scores were
     recorded by individuals who had recently cut-down or stopped, or who
     had never smoked. Individuals who had recently started or increased
     their smoking, and those whose consumption remained unchanged in
     1987, had significantly lower mean HFC scores.
v.   The relationship between HFC and alcohol consumption was similar
     in so far as the highest scores were recorded by respondents who had
     recently reduced their drinking. However, the individuals who report-
     ed that they "never" consumed alcohol had the lowest mean HFC
     scores. Moderate and reduced use of alcohol rather than complete
     abstinence was associated with the highest levels of HFC.

The kind of health and fitness consciousness that our sample exhibited was encouraging the individuals concerned to do positively health-seeking things rather than to refrain from potentially harmful activities, except smoking. Their values were not terrifying our sample into sheltering in their homes to avoid contagion and injury. Quite the reverse; we shall explain later that their leisure was typically rich and active. Most were drinking alcohol (usually in moderation), enjoying meals out (while trying to select healthy menus), entertaining at home, and pursuing a wide range of other leisure interests.

We can test whether HFC, which was measured in 1987, was operating as a causal factor in our sample's lifestyles because the respondents were re-interviewed in 1988 and questioned about whether they had made further changes in the types of behaviour that were covered in the 1987 interviews. This enables us to check whether individuals who achieved high HFC scores in 1987 were the most likely to make subsequent health-seeking changes in their lifestyles during 1988. This is a rather stringent test of the power of health and fitness values, firstly because 12 months is a rather short period in which to expect major lifestyle changes, and secondly because most of those with high HFC scores in 1987 would have needed to improve upon lifestyles that were already exceptionally health seeking. In the event, high HFC in

Figure 10.2

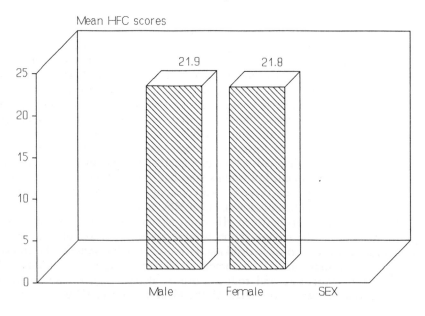

1987 proved unrelated to changes in the sample's sport activity during 1988: those who increased and reduced their activity had almost identical HFC scores. Also, those who increased their smoking during 1988 had a slightly higher mean HFC than those who reduced. However, high HFC in 1987 was related, once again, to reduced alcohol consumption during 1988, and to individuals making an above-average number of other health-seeking changes in their everyday lifestyles. Maybe short-term changes in smoking and sport behaviour had been less responsive to the individuals' own values than to opportunities and constraints – changes in employment and domestic circumstances, new facilities opening, and the spread of no-smoking zones for example. Our evidence on lifestyle changes between 1987 and 1988 is ambiguous, but it offers some indications of sample members with high HFC shaping their lifestyles accordingly.

Within our sample there was no statistically significant sex difference in HFC scores which is quite remarkable given the usually pervasive influence of sex roles and identities (see Figure 10.2). The oldest and the youngest age groups had the lowest mean HFC scores while those aged 25-34 scored highest (Figure 10.3). However, the only statistically significant difference by age was between the over-65s and respondents aged 25-44. Again, it is quite surprising that there were no greater and linear differences given the social, psychological and physiological changes that normally accompany ageing. There was a linear relationship between HFC and occupational class within our sample. The professional and managerial group had the highest mean score, while non-skilled manual workers scored lowest. The range of variation in HFC by occupational class was almost as wide as between non-participants and respondents with the highest levels of sport activity. However, controlling for occupational class did not lead to the disappearance of any of the previously identified relationships between HFC and lifestyle. Within both the middle and working classes, respondents with above-average HFC had the higher rates of sport participation (see Figure 10.4), took more additional forms of exercise, were the more likely to have made recent health-seeking changes in their everyday lives, had the healthier diets, were the more likely to have never smoked, and to have reduced their alcohol consumption up to 1987. Moreover, on most of these lifestyle variables including sport participation, the contrasts between respondents with high and low HFC were much wider than between the middle and working classes overall. There is independent evidence that, given equal opportunity, encouragement and motivation manual workers are just as likely as white-collar employees to make health-seeking changes in their everyday ways of life (Tregoning et al, 1990).

Our evidence does not enable us to identify the origins or primary source of health and fitness consciousness. It is possible that sport was one milieu where this consciousness was being nurtured and transmitted to new participants. Unlike the other health promoting practices associated with this consciousness, sport was drawing like-minded individuals together and it is

Figure 10.3

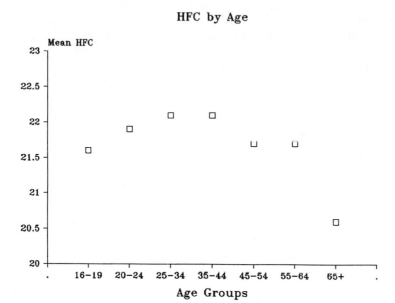

Figure 10.4

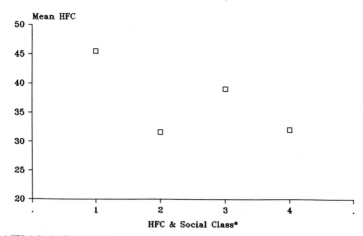

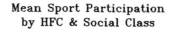

* HFC & Social Class Groups:
1 Hi & Middle   3 Hi & Working
2 Lo & Middle   4 Lo & Working

likely that any distinctive value orientations that they possessed would have been reinforced. However, our research was insufficiently longitudinal to explore the emergence of this type of consciousness. What our evidence shows is that, once acquired, HFC was increasing the likelihood of individuals playing sport and engaging in other kinds of health promoting behaviour, which is not to say that it was a sufficient cause of sport participation or anything else. As previous chapters explained, sustained sport participation in adulthood was only likely if the foundations had been laid when individuals were young. Also, it would be misleading to given the impression that the lifestyles even of respondents with the highest levels of HFC were governed primarily by the pursuit of fitness and health.

A harried leisure class

Gratton and Tice (1989) have previously shown that the main difference between the overall leisure habits of sport players and the remainder of the adult population in Britain is that somehow the former manage to do much more. Their analysis of the leisure evidence collected in Great Britain's General Household Survey (GHS) has shown that sport participants have well-above average participation rates in most other kinds of leisure. Those involved do not appear to play sport at the expense of other leisure activities. To this our evidence adds that the adults in our sample who played sport very frequently had higher participation rates in other leisure activities than less frequent players, and that when individuals increased their sport activity they typically increased their involvement in other forms of leisure simultaneously.

These statements may sound implausible. If people devote considerable time, money and energy to sport, then, it may appear to follow, they must have less for other things. The reality, however, is that life and leisure are not so straight-forward. It is possible for people to make greater use of their time, squeezing more activities into a given number of hours. Having a drink, meeting friends, playing indoor soccer and then a game of snooker can be blended together in a single evening's leisure. A multiplier-effect appears to operate in recreation whereby any initial activities or social relationships tend to generate others. Once individuals "go out" and meet other people they are likely to be introduced to new leisure opportunities. Finding spare time is unlikely to be an intractable problem for most people. In 1990 the typical British adult watched television for over 20 hours per week. These hours, and also time devoted to self-maintenance – washing, cleaning, preparing food, resting and sleeping – can usually contract without any great sacrifice when individuals face other demands. Just as time can be enriched with more activity, it is possible for individuals to manage their finances more carefully and thereby make their money go further. Television sets, videos, compact disc players, cars and clothing can be replaced less frequently, and holidays can be taken at budget prices.

In 1970 Linder coined the term "the harried leisure class" whose growth, he claimed, was an inevitable consequence of spending power increasing more rapidly than time available for consumption. In all industrial societies there has been a trend towards paid employment accounting for a diminishing proportion of lifetime. This trend is commonly regarded as a necessary condition for a growth of leisure. However, Linder drew attention to the fact that personal incomes in the advanced industrial societies have risen even more sharply than leisure time. An inescapable consequence, according to Linder, is that time becomes an increasingly scarce resource. So we begin to place a higher monetary value on our time. We require higher pay than in the past to draw us into the labour market, and we expect premium rates for overtime and unsocial hours. Also, Linder argues, we become anxious to ensure that our precious time is not wasted. Rather than there being a trend towards more relaxed and, in this sense, more leisurely living, Linder argues that leisure is becoming harried. Individuals who work relatively long hours earning relatively high incomes are extreme samples of this predicament. Some critics of the trend allege that it is leading towards the antithesis of true leisure. Godbey (1975) argues that as time becomes increasingly scarce we tend to seek forms of pleasure in which satisfactions can be snatched quickly – short games of squash rather than day-long cricket matches for example.

The lifestyles of the sport participants in our research make an excellent case study of harried leisure. Their sporting interests were typically making heavy demands upon the individuals' time, but the majority were somehow managing to do many additional things besides. For most participants, particularly the more frequent participants, playing sport was just one component in their generally busy leisure lives.

Leisure changes, 1986-1988

We asked identical questions about general leisure behaviour in the 1986 facility surveys and in our 1988 home interviews. These questions were drawn from the General Household Survey (GHS) in which, every two or three years since 1973, nationally representative samples have been asked about their involvement in leisure activities. Respondents are presented with checklists to jog their memories, and are asked to say which of the named activities they took part in just once, or more than once during the previous four weeks. This is the type of question with which the GHS measures sport participation. In our surveys we used more detailed questions to explore this area of leisure, but we adopted the GHS format to measure involvement in other kinds of recreation. We enquired about participation in 21 activities apart from sport, some normally home-based such as gardening and reading, and others out-of-home including visits to the seaside, parks, pubs, historic buildings, for meals out, and to see friends. In 1986 this battery of questions was answered by most of the 4554 respondents in the facility surveys, and in

1988 by most of the 1275 members of the panel who were interviewed at home. Altogether 808 individuals answered these questions satisfactorily on both occasions, so we can measure changes in their leisure behaviour over the two year period.

The vast majority of these individuals were regular sport participants throughout, and among this group there had been a general upward trend in other kinds of leisure activity. There were more increasers than decreasers in 18 out of the 21 non-sport activities on our checklist, the exceptions being do-it-yourself, visits to the cinema, theatre, ballet, concerts and such-like, and watching sport. The more substantial increases were in the proportions who reported entertaining at home (up from 64 percent to 73 percent), visiting other people's homes (81 to 90 percent), and making trips to parks (43 to 53 percent). The mean number of activities in which the sample had taken part during the previous four weeks rose from around nine in 1986 to around ten in 1988, and the mean proportion of all their activities in which the individuals participated more than once a month rose from 64 to 68 percent. The sample's leisure activity had expanded marginally in both range and frequency.

The most likely explanation for the range and frequency of leisure activity rising within our sample is that these individuals were part of a nationwide upward trend in leisure participation in the late-1980s. Leisure was then one of the UK economy's most buoyant sectors. During the economic recovery following the recession of the early-1980s, consumer spending ran ahead of rising domestic output. Hence the widening trade gap. Reductions in income tax and mortgage interest rates during 1986-88 gave the consumer boom additional impetus which was arrested only in 1989 after our fieldwork had been completed. Between 1986 and late-1988 the UK was spending more on in-home and out-of-home leisure, and our recreationally active sample was obviously part of this trend.

As regards sport activity, the overall trend in our sample during the research was towards the individuals playing less rather than more frequently. Unlike the rise in other kinds of leisure activity, this decline in sport participation by our respondents is most easily explained in terms of the composition of the sample. A third of the respondents were aged 16-24 at the beginning of the research in 1986, so the panel that was followed-up in 1987 and 1988 was well-stocked with the age-group within which the decline in sport activity is steepest. One would expect any study which followed the same individuals over several years, particularly in this age-group, to record an overall decline in sport participation. This is an age effect rather than a sign of historical change in social patterns. Also, our initial sample was well-stocked with very frequent players. Such individuals are inevitably well-represented when the chances of being included in a study increase the more frequently individuals visit sport facilities. Whereas non-participants can only change upwards, very frequent players have plenty of scope to reduce their sport activity. These will be the main reasons for the overall decline in sport participation by our sample. The reduction in sport activity was a different kind of trend, and was certainly neither a cause nor a condition for the respondents' increased involvement in other kinds of leisure.

There was an overall decline in sport participation, but our sample contained some individuals who increased, and others, a rather larger number, who reduced their activity. Our most precise measurements are of changes in sport participation between 1987 and 1988, the years when we gathered sufficient information about all the sports that the individuals played, and the frequency, to calculate overall participation scores. When we divide the sample according to whether their sport participation scores increased or declined between 1987 and 1988, and compare trends in these groups' involvement in other kinds of leisure over the same period, we find that more of both the sport increasers and decreasers had expanded than reduced their other leisure activities (see Table 10.1). This applied among men and women in all age groups, but within nearly all these sub-groups the strongest growth in other forms of leisure participation was among the individuals who increased their sport activity. Increased sport participation by our respondents tended to have been accompanied by an above-average widening of the range, and by an above-average increase in the frequency of their involvement in other kinds of leisure.

Table 10.1 *Changes in Sport and Leisure Participation*

	Change in sport participation (1987-1988)	
	Increased	Reduced
Change in Leisure Participation (1986-1988)		
Increased	64%	55%
Same	6%	9%
Reduced	30%	37%
n =	294	386

Maybe it taxes credibility that people with busy leisure lives to begin with could nevertheless find the time to play more sport, to add new forms of recreation to their lifestyles, and to do some of these things more frequently than before. Clearly, there must be a point at which time is filled to capacity, and beyond which people simply cannot find the money or energy to do more of anything without there being compensating sacrifices. The plain fact, however, seems to be that the bulk of Britain's adult population is nowhere near this point. According to our evidence, even the busier sections of the population such as we studied are able to find the time, money and energy to do more if they are sufficiently motivated. We are confident that our findings would be repeated if, rather than sport participants, we initially focused on people with hobbies, who visited the theatre, or went for meals-out frequently. They would be shown to be taking part in more additional leisure activities (including sport) than the remainder of the population. Leisure polarisation is not just a sporting phenomenon. Some people manage to use their leisure to do a lot whereas others do relatively little of anything. And most of the former group appear to retain sufficient slack in their lifestyles to do even more given the opportunity and incentive.

In 1988 all the current participants were asked whether playing sport had affected other areas of their lives. Only 33 percent reported such effects which may seem a surprisingly small figure given sport's time demands. The most likely explanation is that sport had occupied a prominent position in most participants' leisure since their school-days, and other areas of their lives had developed around the demands of sport. Those who reported effects mostly referred to other leisure activities, friends and families, and it is interesting to compare the nature of these effects. Among the families reported to have been affected, only 20 percent were said to be sharing more time with the participants while 80 percent were reported to be receiving less attention. In contrast, 76 percent of participants who reported that other leisure activities had been affected claimed to be doing more rather than less. Similarly, in 82 percent of the cases where friendships were mentioned it was claimed that these had been enriched or widened. Our sample's views are consistent with our more objective evidence; sport participation was tending to enlarge rather than reduce other leisure activities and relationships.

Balanced leisure

Most of our sample were regular sport participants, and our analysis has focused on this particular aspect of their leisure. However, any impression that sport was most of the players' most significant use of leisure needs to be corrected. In the section of the 1988 interviews dealing with general leisure behaviour, respondents were asked to list the three activities that they had enjoyed most, on which they had spent the most money, and to which they had devoted most time during the previous four weeks. Everyone was restricted to our 21 general leisure activities drawn from the GHS, plus sport, so watching television, relaxing, and doing nothing in particular were ruled-out. The sample placed the activities in almost identical rank orders of importance in terms of time, enjoyment and money. It may have been a mistake to ask these questions one after the other in so far as an intention was to discover discrepancies between the importance of activities measured in these three ways. Most respondents simply reeled-off the same answers to each question. The resulting rank order, therefore, is probably best treated as a general indicator of the uses of leisure that the sample judged most important to them. Going out for a drink was the most popular choice followed by meals out, then sport. These were followed by visiting friends and relatives, listening to records and tapes, reading books, and entertaining in the respondents' own homes. Our sample's lifestyles were certainly not austere and puritanical; drinking and eating headed their leisure priorities. Sport was just one activity in their generally full and wide-ranging leisure lives.

In 1987 the sample was asked which of the following was most important to them: enjoying life from day to day (chosen by 45 percent), spending time with their families (25 percent), keeping fit and healthy (17 percent), having a satisfying job (11 percent), and earning as much money as possible (3 percent). The sample's life values were explored further with another set of questions in 1988. This comprised a list of 24 activities, each of which had to be graded from 0 to 10 in its importance to the respondent. The list included sport and other uses of leisure, but also activities such as "earning as much money as possible" and "spending time with my family". Factor analysis of the sample's answers revealed eight distinct value orientations. One of these was *sport* (watching and playing) and another was *exercise* (keeping fit and healthy, and being involved in demanding and creative leisure). Unsurprisingly, respondents who were the most frequent sport participants had particularly high scores on these values, but they invariably also scored highly on some combination of the others. these were *home life* (spending time at home, with the family, and doing domestic chores), *cultural* (following current affairs and visiting the countryside), *social* (seeing friends, going out for a drink, and entertaining), *media* (watching television and video, playing records, and visiting theatres and other places of entertainment), *self-centred* (relaxing and spending time alone), and *occupational* (earning money and having a satisfying job). These values were not set in zero-sum relationships with each other. There is no logical reason why a person who values home life or sport, for example, should therefore devalue the other activities. Virtually all members of the sample scored highly on a combination of the values, which creates a more accurate picture of the type of people that we studied than our own pre-occupation with sport. Most of the participants valued sport as well as, rather than ahead of other elements in their leisure. For the majority, sport was just one among many demands on their leisure time which had to be balanced. They valued playing sport, taking exercise, and keeping fit and healthy, but not necessarily to any greater extent than they valued their family lives and other leisure activities. ´

The highly active and varied character of the leisure lives in which our sample's sport participation was typically embedded perhaps makes it easier to understand why, among the public at large, players tend to be young, male and middle class. It will not be just the sheer amounts of time and money at individuals' disposal that are crucial but also their ability to control, shape and reshape these resources. Young people who have yet to assume major domestic responsibilities are favourably placed to exercise such control. So are men compared with women because the latter's caring and servicing roles are not normally time-bounded. Professional and managerial occupations where the incumbents are allowed and expected to plan their own and other people's schedules will be more likely to nurture the skills necessary for harried leisure than working class occupational experience of working to instructions and doing as much, but certainly no more than required.

Harried leisure, sport and stress

The returns from the stress scale that was included in the 1987 and 1988 home surveys were more limited than we had expected. The relationships between stress scores and lifestyle variables that affected other health factors were reported briefly in chapter 9. The strongest relationship was a lowering of stress as levels of exercise apart from sport increased. There were also relationships between high stress and healthy diets, and high alcohol consumption. Neither energetic nor non-energetic sport participation was significantly related to stress levels. Nor, we can now add, were overall levels of leisure activity.

We had anticipated stronger and more pervasive relationships between stress levels and uses of leisure. After all, sport is supposed to be stress relieving. By releasing energy and aggression players are supposed to become calmer and more relaxed. Other uses of leisure could also be stress reducing in so far as they perform cathartic functions, expressing otherwise frustrated drives, desires and emotions. Also, the social support obtained through sport and other leisure activities could relieve individuals of pressures otherwise contained within themselves. With hindsight, however, it seems equally likely that the social demands and psychological pressures accompanying any leisure activity could be stress inducing. Also, the pressure on individuals' time could be a source of stress. Maybe both sets of leisure processes operate, some increasing and others reducing stress. This could be an explanation for our failure to discover clearer relationships between sport and other types of leisure participation and stress levels.

It is also possible that stress was sometimes a cause rather than an effect of leisure participation. For example, within our sample high stress was related to healthy dieting. It was also related to the number of steps to improve their health that respondents reported having taken in both 1987 and 1988. In addition, high stress in 1987 was related to increased sport activity during the next 12 months. The most plausible explanation for these relationships is that high stress was prompting the individuals to do things, many things, but particularly things that might improve their condition. Now if some of the things that they did turned out to be stress relieving, maybe with sport for example, the overall result would have been as discovered in both 1987 and 1988 – no cross-sectional relationships whatsoever between stress scores and levels of activity.

There were just two sets of relationships between stress and lifestyle variables which deserve further comment. Firstly, there was the positive relationship between stress and alcohol consumption where it is equally plausible to treat drinking as the causal or dependent variable. The remaining relationship between stress and a set of lifestyle variables is the sole instance where it is most plausible to attribute stress reducing properties to the leisure behaviour. This relationship was unusually resilient, holding up longitudinally as well as cross-sectionally. High levels of general leisure activity were related to high stress scores in 1988, though not to a statistically significant extent. Also, respondents who increased their general leisure participation between 1986 and 1988 were more likely to experience an increase, and less likely to experience a decrease in their stress scores between 1987 and 1988 than those who reduced their general leisure activity. Once again, this relationship was not statistically significant, but the indications were that the effect of an overall increase in leisure activity was to increase stress marginally. This makes it all the more surprising and noteworthy that high levels of *total* sport participation, energetic and non-energetic combined, were related to low stress scores in 1987 and 1988, and these relationships were significant statistically. Also, increased total sport activity between 1987 and 1988 was associated with a fall in mean stress scores. Again, this relationship was statistically significant. It appeared to be a

Figure 10.5

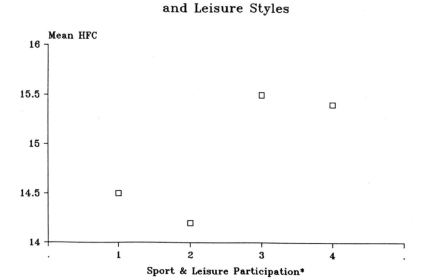

Mean Stress Scores
and Leisure Styles

* Sport & Leisure Participation
1 Hi & Hi   3 Hi & Lo
2 Lo & Hi   4 Lo & Lo

combination of energetic and non-energetic sport activity that was stress relieving. Neither energetic nor non-energetic participation alone had such consequences. It is now worth recalling from chapter 9 that "other exercise" was also related to low stress scores, and that stress scores dipped, though not to a statistically significant extent, at moderate levels of energetic sport activity, roughly three times a week.

Figure 10.5 and Table 10.2 display simultaneously these relationships between stress, overall sport participation, and levels of general leisure activity. The cross-sectional data from 1988 in Figure 10.5 suggests that the best leisure recipe for reducing stress was to play a lot of energetic and non-energetic sport while having few other leisure activities. Table 10.2 describes how stress scores changed between 1987 and 1988 depending on whether individuals' participation in sport and other leisure activities was increasing

Table 10.2 *Changes in sport and leisure activity, and changes in stress*

		Change in sport activity (1987-88)		
		Decrease	Same	Increase
	Decrease	1		2
Change in leisure activity (1986-1988)	Same			
	Increase	3		4

	Group			
	1	**2**	**3**	**4**
Change in stress (1987-88)				
Decrease	40%	51%	39%	41%
Same	17%	19%	15%	21%
Increase	43%	30%	46%	38%
n =	141	87	211	189

or decreasing over the same period. Again, the best leisure formula for lowering stress seems to have been to cut down on other leisure activities while playing more energetic and non-energetic sport.

Why should a high level of sport activity, provided it was composed of energetic and non-energetic games, have had special stress relieving properties? Here we can only speculate. Maybe the degree to which sports are necessarily rule governed relieves participants of pressures that accompany most other leisure activities. Maybe very frequent participation in either energetic or non-energetic sport alone does as much harm as good in stress terms whereas the variety inherent in a balance between the two, supplemented by other exercise, normally far less vigorous than energetic sport, relieves stress.

In view of the sparsity of the relationships between stress and lifestyle variables, and the difficulties faced in interpreting the relationships that were found within our sample, it seems best to conclude that stress must have depended mainly on other factors. There were no relationships within our sample between stress scores and age, sex or socio-economic status, but we certainly cannot rule out the possibility of such relationships being discovered in samples more representative of the general public. It is also likely that by adulthood, and possibly at birth to some extent, basic personality structures are set and thereafter some individuals are destined to be more stressed than others whatever their circumstances and lifestyles. Of course, there are powerful genetic determinants in most of the health factors that we measured. Childhood conditions were also likely to have played some part in fixing our respondents' cardiovascular health, strength and illness freedom. However, these health factors, plus self-assessments, were clearly capable of modification by appropriate lifestyles whereas in the case of stress this did not apply to anything like the same or as clear an extent.

11

CONCLUSIONS

Chapter one emphasised how this research was intended to be socially useful rather than a purely academic exercise. We wanted to establish more precisely than ever before the personal costs and benefits, especially in health and fitness terms, arising from the types of sport activity that take place in the local authority and voluntary centres, and the private clubs, that are now accessible to, and used by hundreds of thousands of ordinary members of the public across the country. We also wanted to learn more, not only about why only some adults remain sports-active, but in particular the circumstances under which participation would rise within various sections of the population defined by age, sex and socio-economic status. Plainly speaking, we wanted to establish whether sport for all was a realistic objective, and whether the likely health benefits would be worth the effort.

Now a problem always inherent in research that advances beyond what was formerly known is that the findings cannot be predicted confidently. So if the policy implications arising from previous chapters are less than crystal clear this will not necessarily mean that the research was either defective or unsuccessful. We would have preferred to conclude with strong and clear policy recommendations; in the event we find ourselves able to marshall the evidence equally persuasively to support, then to criticise the health case for sport.

The health case for sport

On the positive side, we found, firstly, that playing sport really was conferring health benefits which included but went beyond making the participants feel healthier and fitter. Participation was also related to high scores on the health factor that we have called strength, which was indicated mainly by the measurements of muscular power and lung function. Secondly, these benefits were being experienced by ordinary members of the public who were using sports centres in ways typical of such participants. They were not all elite athletes, though a minority were very good at their best sports, and they were not prescribed a training regime specifically devised to improve health and fitness. Our's was not an experimental study using a group of exceptionally motivated volunteers. Nor were we promoting or piloting a scientifically devised schedule for boosting health-related fitness. Rather, we studied ordinary sports centre users who were playing in the ways that such people ordinarily do. Thirdly, the health benefits of sport participation were evident within all socio-demographic groups; male and female, young and old, employed and not employed, and rich and poor. In terms of the types and levels of health benefits conferred, sport was proving equally good for everyone. Fourthly, the health benefits of sport were additional to any that were being experienced as a result of other favourable lifestyle practices. They were being enjoyed by people who would probably have been in good health in any case, and by others whose benefits were obtained from lower starting points. Individuals who were initially unfit were improving their health through sport, and so were individuals who were already fit and healthy for their age and sex. Sport participation was certainly not the sole determinant of these people's health, but however favourable or unfavourable their other circumstances and living habits, playing sport was leading to measurable gains. There were no groups whose conditions were either so hopeless or so advantaged to begin with that they could derive no health benefits from sport.

An obvious use of this evidence is to push sport to the fore in health promotion. Here is a pastime that really can improve everyone's health. It does not need to be promoted selectively. Unlike some other medicines it is an activity that the participants actually enjoy. Pursuing health through sport does not involve persuading people to desist from behaviour that they find pleasurable. Rather, health promotion through sport can work with the grain, and our evidence on the structure of sport careers shows how lifetime sport for all could be made into a reality. We found that people were likely to remain in sport throughout adulthood if they became proficient in several games when young then continued to play during the crucial life-phase of young adulthood when they were leaving education, changing their residences, establishing themselves in employment, forming new households, and embarking upon parenthood. Our evidence shows clearly that the foundations for lifelong sport participation were typically laid early in life. Hence the case for enriching sport curricula in schools with multiple timetabled sessions each week and opportunities to play many different games. The complementary need will be for low cost (to the users) but high quality community facilities where the playing conditions, changing accommodation and social provisions attract and retain young (and older) adults. The adults among whom sport participation is currently highest, namely, males in the professional and management strata, especially those who benefit from higher education, typically spend young adulthood in environments where sport is readily accessible. Why not extend the same opportunities to all? Why not make sport centre programmes and facilities as appealing to females as to males, and ensure that all young adults have the same sport opportunities as those who continue in post-compulsory education? Of course, someone will have to provide the resources, but the strategy is neither socially unrealistic nor economically impossible in an increasingly prosperous country, and the investment can be justified on leisure and health grounds.

A sceptical reply

A problem with our evidence is that it can be raided to construct an equally persuasive case against reliance on sport in health promotion. Firstly, sport participation was not impacting directly on all the health factors that we were able to distinguish. It was improving the participants' self-assessments and strength, but not their cardiovascular health or illness freedom. Moreover, at low levels of sport activity, less than three times a week, only self-assessments showed statistically significant and consistent improvements within all socio-demographic groups. One might argue that just making people feel healthier is worthwhile in itself, and that this may lead to desirable secondary consequences; that individuals who feel healthier and fitter will then engage in other types of health promoting activity. However, it is also possible that individuals who feel healthier after their weekly swims or games of squash will thereafter feel less need to control other aspects of their lifestyles. In any case, sport was not proving uniquely capable of improving self-assessed health and fitness. Adopting any type of behaviour that the individuals believed to be health promoting seemed to have this effect. A weakness in the health case for sport is that a combination of other lifestyle practices would impact on a wider range of health factors and thereby lead to a more comprehensive improvement. Specifically, attention to diet, avoidance of tobacco and regular or heavy drinking would lead to gains in self-assessments, strength, cardiovascular health and illness freedom. There was no sign whatsoever in our evidence of playing sport leading to the types of health improvement that would reduce the participants' need for medical care. Illness freedom was not among the health factors that were responding to sport activity. If more people who were unhealthy to begin with had been playing sport and had therefore appeared in our sample, participation might have reduced their vulnerability to illnesses. However, the types of people who played sport were remaining just as vulnerable as otherwise to illnesses, infections, accidents and injuries. In one respect their vulnerability increased since sports injuries had been quite common. Also, needless to say, playing sport could not reduce the participants' risks of parenting children with congenital disabilities, nor prevent the players themselves from becoming terminally ill eventually. Given that priorities are unavoidable in a world of scarce resources, an argument against backing sport in health campaigns, particularly if an aim is to reduce demands on medical services and budgets, is that other lifestyle practices would make a more powerful all-round impact.

A second weakness in the case for sport is that, even alongside other favourable lifestyle practices, it was not eliminating or even reducing the health inequalities associated with age, sex and socio-economic status. Sport was improving the health of all socio-demographic groups, but it was not ironing out the inequalities between them. This means that in so far as an aim of health promotion is to draw the less healthy sections of the population towards the norm, sport will not be an effective vehicle. Moreover, for the reasons given in previous chapters, sport participation remains most common among relatively healthy sections of the population, namely, the upper middle classes. Also, the middle classes were proving the more likely to derive health benefits from favourable lifestyle practices. If all other things remained equal, therefore, indiscriminately encouraging and assisting everyone to stay-in or restart in sport would be more likely to widen than to narrow socio-economic health inequalities.

A third weakness in the case for sport concerns whether it is realistic, in practice as opposed to theory, even over a generation or more, to envisage all or even most adults playing enough energetic sport to achieve more than improvements in their self-assessed health and fitness. The responsiveness of self-assessments to minor changes in sport activity explains why sport sessions can attract streams of newcomers who quickly express satisfaction that their health and fitness are benefiting. We noted earlier that restarts among the formerly inactive tended to be temporary. This means that those concerned were unlikely to derive any benefits in physical health. Moving into and out of occasional sport activity will reward individuals with repeated feelings that they are improving their condition, but no other health gains are likely. Our evidence is entirely congruent with the recommendation of the American College of Sports Medicine (1990) that maintaining fitness in healthy adults requires vigorous exercise on three or four days each week. Our evidence concurs that sport participation needs to be energetic and frequent to achieve changes in physical functioning. Improving one's health through sport is hard work. Weekly swimming is insufficient. Moreover, to retain the full health benefits individuals need to continue to participate several times a week throughout their lifetimes. Building this level of sport activity into the typical adult's lifestyle will be a formidable task. The goal might be sociologi-cally and economically feasible in the long-term, if it was made a top priority. If sport was treated as a priority in schools, and if community facilities were sufficiently plentiful and attractive to persuade as many young adults as possible to continue to play while leaving room for the next generation, we are confident that adult participation would rise steadily. However, in practice we know that school timetables and budgets are overloaded with competing demands. We also know that there is heavy competition for central and local government resources. Likewise, there is enormous compe-tition for everyone's leisure time and money. This suggests that relying on sport to improve the public's health will be a high risk strategy. Simply broadcasting the message that sport is health promoting will achieve little. Most people already agree. Indeed, if anything they probably over-estimate the health benefits of modest levels of sport activity.

A niche for sport

The balance of all the evidence and arguments, in our view, points towards a niche rather than a foundation role for sport within health policy and promotion. It is easy to over-play the health case for sport. Enthusiasts are probably too easily convinced, and likewise those seeking low cost solutions to health problems and inequalities. Ingham (1985) has criticised the entire debate on lifestyles and health for diverting attention from structural impediments to people's well-being, suggesting that individuals can solve their own health problems and, by implication, that unhealthy groups have only themselves to blame for their predicaments.

At the time of our research in the 1980s the UK had a government that was committed to reducing public spending and spreading an "enterprise culture". People were being encouraged to "get on", to make and keep more of their own money so as to be able to provide for their own pensions, dental care, eye tests and so on. There was incontrovertible evidence of relatively low and, in some cases, actually declining health in certain regions and social groups adversely affected by the decade's socio-economic polarisation (Townsend et al, 1988). Members of an otherwise apparently uncaring government could disclaim responsibility by asserting that people's well-being depended on lifestyles that were under their own control, and that the sources of their poor health lay not in disadvantaged groups' unemployment, low incomes or poor housing so much as in what they ate, drank and smoked.

The policy implications arising from our evidence and analysis are wholly at loggerheads with the UK's dominant political ideology of the 1980s. Firstly, our evidence suggests that lifestyles are not the basic source of health inequalities between socio-demographic groups. Even when economically disadvantaged groups were making the healthiest of all possible leisure choices, their well-being remained handicapped by their low incomes, relatively poor housing and working conditions, and vulnerability to unemployment. Secondly, our evidence suggests strongly that a condition for promoting health through sport will be public investment in additional facilities. The past rise of sport participation in the UK rested on such public investment and it is difficult to see how the trend could continue without increased support from central and local government. Thirdly, it may well be the case that if and when improvements in living and working conditions remove former sources of ill-health, and as medical science and services offer relief from a growing number of ailments and injuries, lifestyles will increase in importance as sources of variation in levels of health, and will be the main means whereby people can actually control their own well-being. But this will never justify removing the underlying props, the medical services, economic, income maintenance and labour market policies on which past progress depended.

Some of Ingham's criticisms are directed at sport and health researchers who have been willing to place the most favourable possible interpretations upon any fragments of evidence, and who have naively propagated their convictions appearing to believe that the facts need only to be made widely known for mass changes in lifestyles to be effected. We hope that our research is not vulnerable to these particular criticisms. It is unsafe to assume that the health and fitness gains recorded in experimental studies, and with elite groups of athletes, are being achieved, even on a reduced scale, by the everyday users of public sport facilities. It is insufficient to show that sport participants are generally healthier than non-players on virtually all indicators. Other potential influences on health need to be taken into account. Allowance must also be made for ill-health keeping people out, rather than arising from their lack of sport activity. Demonstrating that correlations are genuine sport effects means looking for step-by-step improvements as participation rises, and preferably establishing a temporal sequence. Once these controls and checks are introduced, clear benefits from sport participation remain apparent, though they are probably less extensive, and require higher and more sustained levels of commitment to sport than may have been hoped.

The health promoting case for sport is certainly not total fabrication. Even so, we must agree with Ingham that great health expectations of sport need to be deflated on scientific and health grounds. Sport is no health solve-all. Its impact is focused on a limited number of health factors, and it offers no solution to socio-economic health inequalities. If sport for all remains unrealisable even in the long-term, our evidence suggests that this will be a health handicap rather than a disaster. Sedentary as opposed to active lifestyles will certainly pull general health levels beneath the heights that would otherwise be possible given that the benefits of all lifestyle practices seem to be additive with none compensating for the absence of others. Nevertheless, a combination of healthy diets, moderate if any alcohol consumption, and avoidance of tobacco will operate on a larger number of health factors than sport participation alone. Reducing economic inequalities will have similar comprehensive health effects. In terms of the health implications, low sport participation is not the worst of all possibilities. Since our research was conducted a national fitness survey has measured the fitness and lifestyles of a representative sample of British adults. The results of this enquiry suggest in that 1990 only six percent of adults were taking sufficient exercise to achieve and maintain full fitness (Rowe, 1991). If this estimate is correct, the majority of the 45 percent or so of adults who were sport participants according to Sports Council estimates, could not have been playing with sufficient intensity or regularity to improve their physical health. It is possibly realistic to envisage raising the proportion of the adult population that obtains physical health benefits from sport to 10 or 12 percent over a decade or generation, but this will hardly be an answer to the nation's health problems since around 90 percent will still be deriving no benefits from the strategy.

If either the facilities or the sports education in childhood and youth that would be necessary to realise sport for all cannot be delivered, the best use of more limited sport resources, on health grounds, will probably be more-or-less as at present, that is, frequent and persistent use by a minority who therefore obtain most of the potential health benefits, rather than spasmodic or infrequent use by larger numbers, few of whom would gain more, in health terms, than simply feeling better. It appears that the present pattern of adult sport participation in Britain – very frequent play by a few and hardly any by the rest – is actually the best formula at current levels of resourcing and activity for maximising the public health benefits. While this pattern of participation persists, the best niche for sport in health promotion will be to concentrate on retaining existing players, encouraging them to persist and to participate at the frequency necessary to maximise the health benefits. In other words, the target groups will be the young and older adults who have remained in sport. Preaching to the converted is probably the best strategy, purely on health grounds, while sport for all remains a distant prospect.

This suggests that sport should be cautious in adopting health objectives. Sport deserves a niche, but no more, in health policy, and likewise, in our view, health objectives merit only a niche in sport promotion. Some adults play sport mainly for health reasons, but a larger number treat the potential health gains as just one of several sets of benefits from playing. For many players any health and fitness benefits are just a happy accident. Most of the participants that we studied were in sport basically because they had enjoyed the activities since childhood and wanted to continue doing so. They enjoyed the sociability, the physical and mental exertion, and competing against opponents, their own past performances or self-set targets. Even those with a well-developed health and fitness consciousness normally had additional, and usually stronger leisure and life objectives. Paradoxically, sport is likely to maximise its contribution to public health by keeping para-medical personnel and arguments in the background. We have no doubt that the most success-ful marketing of sport will be as recreation, not as a branch of medicine. Sport is likely to be a double loser if it stakes its claims for the nation's time and money on its health promoting properties. Firstly, other methods of health promotion will be shown to be more effective, actually and potentially, in improving the health of larger numbers of people. Secondly, sport will neglect the majority of its actual and potential participants for whom health benefits are neither the main goal nor effect. Is it in the sport's interest, or the general public interest, to concentrate more sports publicity and resources on the 10 percent or so of the adult population who can be realistically expected to play regularly and frequently? There are larger numbers of participants who derive different benefits. There are many other adults who could enjoy the leisure experience of sport but who are currently non-participants. Should the interests of these much larger groups take second place in sports policy to what is likely to remain the much smaller number of very frequent players?

BIBLIOGRAPHY

American Alliance for Health, Physical Education, Recreation and Dance (1986), *The Value of Physical Activity,* AAHPERD, Reston, Virginia.

American College of Sports Medicine (1990), 'The recommended quantity and quality of exercise for developing and maintaining cardiorespiratory and muscular fitness in healthy adults', *Medicine and Science in Sports and Exercise,* 22, 265-274.

Archer, J. and M. McDonald (1990), 'Gender roles and sports in adolescent girls', *Leisure Studies,* 9, 225-240.

Audit Commission (1989), *Sport for Whom? Clarifying the Local Authority Role in Sport and Recreation,* HMSO, London.

Aylon, A., O. Inbar and O. Bar-Or (1974), 'Relationships among measurements of explosive strength and anaerobic power', in R C Nelson and C A Morehouse, eds, *Biomechanics IV,* University Park Press, Baltimore.

Bacon, W. (1990), 'Gatekeepers of public leisure: a case study of executive leisure managers in the UK', *Leisure Studies,* 9, 71-89.

Bailey, C. and B. Biddle (1988), 'Community health-related physical fitness testing and the National Garden Festival Health Fair at Stoke-on-Trent', *Health Promotion Journal,* 47, 144-147.

Barrell, G., A. Chamberlain, J. Evans, T. Holt and J. MacKean (1989), 'Ideology and commitment in family life: the case of runners', *Leisure Studies,* 8, 249-262.

Bassey, J. and P.H. Fentem (1981), *Exercise: The Facts,* Oxford University Press, Oxford.

Belloc, N.B. and L. Breslow (1972), 'Relationship of health status and health practices', *Preventive Medicine,* 1, 409-421.

Bishop, J. and P. Hoggett (1986), *Organizing Around Enthusiasms,* Comedia, London.

Blaxter, M. (1985), 'Self-definition of health status and consulting rates in primary care', *The Quarterly Journal of Social Affairs,* 1, 131-171.

Blaxter, M. (1987), 'Self-reported health', in B.D. Cox et al, *The Health and Lifestyle Survey,* Health Promotion Research Trust, London.

Blaxter, M. (1990), *Health and Lifestyles,* Tavistock/Routledge, London.

Boothby, J., M. Tungatt, A.R. Townsend and M.F. Collins (1981), *A Sporting Chance?* Sports Council Study 22, London.

Bray, G.A. (Ed), 1979, *Obesity in America,* Proceedings of the 2nd Fogarty International Centre Conference on Obesity, No. 79, US DHEW, Washington.

Brettschneider, W.D. (1990), 'Adolescents, leisure, sport and life-style', paper presented to *AIESEP* Conference, Loughborough University.

Brodie, D.A., L.P. Asturias de Cuevas, K.L. Lamb and K. Roberts (1990), 'Sports injuries amongst indoor sport participants', paper presented to *World Congress on Sport for All,* Tampere, June 4 - 7.

Brodie, D.A., K.L. Lamb and K. Roberts (1988a), 'Body composition and self-perceived health and fitness among indoor sports participants', *Ergonomics*, 31, 1551-1557.

Brodie, D.A., K.L. Lamb and K. Roberts (1988b), 'Health, fitness and body composition of indoor sports participants', poster presented at the *International Conference on Exercise, Fitness and Health*, Toronto, May 29-June 3.

Brown, D.R. (1990), 'Exercise, fitness and mental health', in C. Bouchard, R.J. Shepard et al, eds, *Exercise, Fitness and Health: A Concensus of Current Knowledge*, Human Kinetics, Illinois.

Brown, J.S. and M. Rawlinson (1975), 'Relinquishing the sick role following open-heart surgery', *American Journal of Epidemiology*, 16, 12-27.

Centre for Leisure Research (1985), *Glasgow Leisure Survey: Attitudes to Provision for Sport*, Dunfermline College of Physical Education.

Chave, S.P.W., J.N. Morris and S. Moss (1978), 'Vigorous exercise in leisure-time and the death rate: a study of male civil servants', *Journal of Epidemiology and Community Health*, 32, 239-243.

Chick, G. and J.M. Roberts (1989), 'Leisure and antileisure in game play', *Leisure Sciences*, 11, 73-84.

Chisolm, D.M. et al (1975), 'Physical activity readiness', *British Columbia Medical Journal*, 17, 375-378.

City of Glasgow Parks and Recreation Department (1985), *A City Recreation Plan*, Glasgow.

Coalter, F. (1986), *Rationale for Public Sector Involvement in Leisure*, Sports Council/ESRC, London.

Cockerham, W.C., K. Sharp and J.A. Wilcox (1983), 'Ageing and perceived health status', *Journal of Gerontology*, 38, 349-355.

Cox, B.D., M. Blaxter, A.L.J. Buckle et al (1987), *The Health and Lifestyle Survey*, Health Promotion Research Trust, London.

Crombie, I.C., A.J. Lee, W.C.S. Smith and H. Tunstall-Pedoe (1990), 'Levels and social patterns of self-reported physical activity in Scotland', *Health Education Journal*, 45, 71-74.

Deem, R. (1982), 'Women, leisure and inequality', *Leisure Studies*, 1, 29-46.

Deem, R. (1986), *All Work and No Play?* Open University Press, Milton Keynes.

Dempsey, K. (1990), 'Women's life and leisure in an Australian rural community', *Leisure Studies*, 9, 35-44.

Dench, S. (1988), 'Women in sport', paper presented to *Leisure Studies Association Conference*, Brighton.

European Atherosclerosis Society Study Group (1987), 'Strategies for the prevention of coronary heart disease: a policy statement of the European Atherosclerosis Society', *European Heart Journal*, 8, 77-88.

Featherstone, M. (1989), 'City cultures and postmodern lifestyles', in Recreatie Reeks Nr 7, *Cities for the Future*, Stichting Recreatie, Den Haag.

Featherstone, M. (1990), 'Perspectives on consumer culture', *Sociology*, 24, 5-22.

Ferraro, K.F. (1980), 'Self-ratings of health among the old and old-old', *Journal of Health and Social Behaviour,* 21, 45-51.

Fillenbaum, G.G. (1980), 'Social content and self-assessment of health among the elderly', *Journal of Health and Social Behaviour,* 20, 45-51.

Fitness Canada (1987), *Standardized Test of Fitness: Assessment Report,* Minister of State, Fitness and Amateur Sport, Canada.

Friedsam, H.J. and H.W. Martin (1963), 'A comparison of self and physicians' health ratings in an older population', *Journal of Health and Social Behaviour,* 4, 179-183.

Furlong, A., R. Campbell and K. Roberts (1989) *Class and Gender Divisions Among Young Adults at Leisure,* Centre for Educational Sociology, University of Edinburgh.

Garrity, T.F. (1973a), 'Social involvement and activeness as predictors of morale six months after first myocardial infarction', *Social Science and Medicine,* 7, 199-207.

Garrity, T.F. (1973b), 'Vocational adjustment after first myocardial infarction', *Social Science and Medicine,* 7, 705-717.

Garrow, J.S. (1981), *Treat Obesity Seriously,* Churchill Livingstone, London.

Glyptis, S. and C. Pack (1988), *Local Authority Sports Provision for the Unemployed,* Sports Council, London.

Godbey, G. (1975), 'Anti-leisure and public recreation policy', in S. Parker et al, eds, *Sport and Leisure in Contemporary Society,* Leisure Studies Association, London.

Goldstein, M.S., J.M. Siegal and R. Boyer (1984), 'Predicting changes in perceived health status', *American Journal of Public Health,* 74, 611-614.

Gratton, C. (1984), 'Public subsidies to leisure', *Leisure Management,* 4, 10, 10-11 and 20.

Gratton, C. and P. Taylor (1987), 'Why provide? Management objectives in leisure', *Leisure Management,* 7, 1, 23-25.

Gratton, C. and A. Tice (1989), 'Sports participation and health', *Leisure Studies,* 8, 77-92.

Greater London Council (1986), *A Sporting Chance,* London.

Green, E., S. Hebron and D. Woodward (1987), *Leisure and Gender,* ESRC/ Sports Council, London.

Green, E., S. Hebron and D. Woodward (1990), *Women's Leisure, What Leisure?,* Macmillan, London.

Griffin, C. (1985), *Typical Girls?,* Routledge, London.

Griffiths, G.T. and A.J. Veal (1985), *Leisure Centres - Inner-London,* Polytechnic of North London.

Hantrais, L. (1985), 'Leisure lifestyles and the synchronisation of family schedules: a Franco-British comparative perspective', *World Leisure and Recreation,* 20, 2, 18-24.

Hantrais, L. and T.J. Kamphorst, eds (1987), *Trends in the Arts: a Multinational Perspective,* Giordano Bruno, Amersfoort, The Netherlands.

Heartbeat Wales (1986), *Welsh Heart Health Survey: Clinical Manual,* Heartbeat Wales, Cardiff.

Hedges, B. (1986), *Personal Leisure Histories,* ESRC Sports Council, London.

Hendry, L.B. (1978), *School, Sport and Leisure,* Lepus, London.

Henry, I. (1990), 'Leisure, the local state and the changing economy in Britain', paper presented to *AIESEP* Conference, Loughborough University.

Hockey, R.V. (1977), *Physical Fitness - the Pathway to Healthful Living,* C.V. Mosby, St. Louis.

Holtain Ltd (1988), *User Manual for the Body Composition Analyser,* Holtain, Crosswell, Crymych, Dyfed.

Hunt, S.M., J. McEwen and S.P. McKenna (1985), 'Measuring health status: a new tool for clinicians and epidemiologists', *Journal of the Royal College of General Practitioners,* 35, 185-188.

Hunt, S.M., J. McEwen and S.P. McKenna (1986), *Measuring Health Status,* CroomHelm, Beckenham.

Ingham, I.G. (1985), 'From public issue to personal trouble: well-being and the fiscal crisis of the state', *Sociology of Sport Journal,* 2, 43-55.

Jaakson, R. (1989), 'Recreational boating spatial patterns: theory and management', *Leisure Sciences,* 11, 85-98.

Jette, M. (1978), 'The standardized test of fitness in occupational health: a pilot project', *Canadian Journal of Public Health,* 69, 431-438.

Kamphorst, T.J. and K. Roberts, eds (1989), *Trends in Sport: a Multinational Perspective,* Giordano Bruno, Culemborg.

Kaplan, G.A. and T. Camacho (1983), 'Perceived health and mortality: a nine-year follow-up of the Human Population Laboratory Cohort', *American Journal of Epidemiology,* 117, 292-304.

Kaplan, S.H. (1987), 'Patient reports of health status among the new urban homeless', *Journal of Chronic Diseases,* 40: suppl. 1, 27S-35S.

Keys, A., F. Fidanza, M.J. Karvonen, N. Kimura and H.L. Taylor (1972), 'Indices of relative weight and height', *Journal of Chronic Diseases,* 25, 329-343.

Kilpatrick, R. and K. Trew (1985), 'Lifestyle and well-being among unemployed men in Northern Ireland', *Journal of Occupational Psychology,* 58, 207-216.

Koch-Weser, E. (1990), 'A framework for the quantitative study of leisure styles', paper presented to *International Sociological Association* conference, Madrid.

Koplan, J.P., D.S. Siscovick and G.M. Goldbaum (1985), 'The risks of exercise: a public health view of injuries and hazards', *Public Health Reports,* 100, 189-195.

Lamb, K.L., D.A. Brodie and K. Roberts (1988), 'Physical fitness and health-related fitness as indicators of a positive health state', *Health Promotion* 3, 171-182.

Lamb, K.L., S. Dench, D.A. Brodie and K. Roberts (1988), 'Sports participation and health status: a preliminary analysis', *Social Science and Medi-*

cine, 27, 1309-1316.

Lamb, K.L., K. Roberts and D.A. Brodie (1990), 'Self-perceived health among sports participants and non-sports participants', *Social Science and Medicine*, 29.

LaRue, A.S., L. Bank, L. Jarvik and M. Hetland (1979), 'Health in old age: how do physicians' ratings and self-ratings compare?', *Journal of Gerontology*, 34, 687-691.

Leisure Management (1988), 'The compulsory tendering debate', 8,2,34-39.

Lensky, H. (1988), 'Community in a recreational setting', *Leisure Sciences*, 11, 303-322.

Levy, L. (1989), 'Community in a recreational', *Leisure Sciences*, 11, 303-322.

Linder, S. (1970), *The Harried Leisure Class*, Columbia University Press, New York.

Linn, B.S. and M.W. Linn (1980), 'Objective and self-assessed health in the old and very old', *Social Science and Medicine*, 14A, 311-315.

Liverpool City Council Sport and Recreation Division (1984), *The Recreation Strategy*, Liverpool.

Liverpool Women and Sport Working Party (1987), *Building Bridges: policy document for the Leisure Services Committee on women and girls' participation in sport*, Liverpool City Council, Liverpool.

Lloyd, N. (1985), *Work and Leisure in the 1980s*, ESRC/Sports Council, London.

McAuley, H.C. and K R Hirons (no date), *Sport and Recreation in Northern Ireland*, Polytechnic of North London.

McCusker, J. (1985), 'Involvement of 15-19 year olds in sport and physical activity', paper presented to *Leisure Studies Association* conference, Ilkley.

McGuire, F.A., F.D. Dottavio and J.T. O'Leary (1987), 'The relationship between early life experiences and later life leisure behaviour', *Leisure Sciences*, 9, 251-257.

McIntosh, P. and V. Charlton (1985), *The Impact of Sport for All Policy 1966-1984*, Sports Council, London.

MacIntryre, S. (1986), 'The patterning of health by social position in contemporary Britain: directions for sociological research', *Social Science and Medicine*, 33, 393-415.

Maddox, G.L. (1964), 'Self-assessment of health status: a longitudinal study of selected elderly subjects', *Journal of Chronic Diseases*, 17, 449-460.

Maddox, G.L. and E.B. Douglass (1973), 'Self-assessment of health', *Journal of Chronic Diseases*, 14, 87-93.

Mihalik, B.J., J.T. O'Leary, F.A. McGuire and F.D. Dottavio (1989), 'Sports involvement across the life span: expansion and contraction of sports activities', *Research Quarterly for Exercise and Sport*, 60, 396-398.

Millar, W.J. and T. Stephens (1987), 'The prevalence of overweight and obesity in Britain, Canada and United States', *American Journal of Public Health*, 77, 38-41.

Minten, J. and K. Roberts (1989), 'Sport in Great Britain', in T.J. Kamphorst and K. Roberts, eds, *Trends in Sport, a Multinational Perspective*, Giordano Bruno, Culemborg, The Netherlands.

Mootz, M. (1986), 'Health indicators', *Social Science and Medicine*, 32, 255-263.

Morgan, W.P. (1984), 'The psychological effects of exercise', in *Exercise Health and Medicine: Proceedings of a Symposium*, Sports Council, London.

Morris, J.N., D.G. Clayton, M.G. Everitt, A.M. Semmence and E.H. Burgess (1990), 'Exercise in leisure time: coronary attack and death rates', *British Heart Journal*, 63, 325-334.

Mossey, J.A., E. Mutran, K. Knott and B. Craik (1989), 'Determinants of recovery 12 months after hip fracture', *American Journal of Public Health*, 79, 279-286.

Mossey, J.A. and E. Shapiro (1982), 'Self-rated health: a predictor of mortality among the healthy', *American Journal of Public Health*, 72, 800-808.

Nutbeam, D. (1986), 'Health promotion glossary', *Health Promotion*, 1, 113-127.

Ortho-Gomer, K., A-L. Unden and M.E. Edwards (1988), 'Social isolation and mortality in ischeamic heart disease', *Acta Medica Scandinavica*, 224, 205-215.

Paffenbarger Jr., R.S. and R.T. Hyde (1984), 'Exercise in the prevention of coronary heart disease', *Preventive Medicine*, 13, 3-22.

Paffenbarger Jr., R.S., R.T. Hyde and A.L. Wing (1990), 'Physical activity and physical fitness as determinants of health and longevity', in C. Bouchard et al, eds, *Exercise, Fitness and Health: A Consensus of Current Knowledge*, Human Kinetics, Illinois.

Palta, M., R.J. Prineas and P. Hannan (1982), 'Comparison of self-reported and measured height and weight', *American Journal of Epidemiology*, 115, 223-230.

Pilpel, D., S. Carmel and D. Galinsky (1988), 'Self-rated health among the elderly', *Comparative Gerontology*, 2, 110-116.

Pollack, M.L., D.H. Schmidt and A.S. Jackson (1980), 'Measurement of cardio-respiratory fitness and body composition in the clinical setting', *Comprehensive Therapy*, 6, 12-17.

Prosser, R. (1981), *The Leisure Systems of Advantaged Adolescents*, PhD. thesis, University of Birmingham.

Rayner, M., A. Heugham, G. Pearson and E. Brunner (1990), 'Why don't people living in Hackney take more exercise?' *Health Education Journal*, 45, 64-68.

Roadburgh, A. (1977), *An Enquiry into the Meanings of Work and Leisure*, PhD thesis, University of Edingburgh.

Roberts, K., L. Asturias, R. Campbell, C. Chadwick and D.A. Brodie (1990), 'Health and fitness consciousness and the lifestyles of adult sport participants', paper presented to conference on *The Future of Adult Life*, The Netherlands.

Roberts, K., S. Dench and D. Brodie (1990), 'Leisure styles and the rest of life', in B Filipcova, S Glyptis and W Tokarski, eds, *Life-styles: Theories, Concepts, Methods and the Results of Life-style Research in International Perspective, Vol. II,* Institute for Philosophy and Sociology of the Czechoslovak Academy of Sciences, Prague.

Roberts, K., S. Dench, J. Minten and C. York (1989), *Community Response to Leisure Centre Provision in Belfast,* Sports Council Study 34, London.

Roberts, K., J.H. Minten, C. Chadwick, K.L. Lamb and D.A. Brodie (1990), 'Sporting lives: a case study of leisure careers', paper presented to *Sixth Canadian Conference on Leisure Research,* Waterloo.

Roberts, K., J. Minten and K. Lamb (1987), 'Explaining leisure provisions', paper presented to seminar on *Leisure - the Voluntary and Public Sectors,* Dunfermline College of Physical Education.

Roberts, K., C.S. York and D.A. Brodie (1988), 'Participant sport in the commercial sector', *Leisure Studies,* 7, 145-157.

Robinson, J. and N. Mutrie (1988), 'Converting the couch potato', *Leisure Management,* 9, February, 53-55.

Rojek, C. (1990), 'Baudrillard and leisure', *Leisure Studies,* 9,7-20.

Ross, C. and D. Hayes (1988), 'Exercise and psychologic well-being in the community', *American Journal of Epidemiology,* 127, 762-771.

Royal College of Physicians (1983), 'Obesity: a report of the Royal College of Physicians', *Journal of the Royal College of Physicians,* 17, 5-65.

Rudman, W.J. (1989), 'Age involvement in sport and physical activity', *Sociology of Sport Journal,* 6, 228-246.

Scott, D. and F.K. Willits (1989), 'Adolescent and adult leisure patterns: a 37-year follow-up study', *Leisure Sciences,* 11, 323-335.

Scottish Sports Council (1979), *A Question of Balance, Main Report, Vols I and II,* Edinburgh.

Scraton, S. (1987), 'Boys muscle in where angels fear to tread - girls' sub-cultures and physical activities', in J. Horne, D. Jary and A. Tomlinson, eds, *Sport, Leisure and Social Relations,* Routledge, London.

Shapiro, C.M., P.M. Warren, J. Trinder et al (1984), 'Fitness facilitates sleep', *European Journal of Applied Physiology,* 53, 1-4.

Siegal, S., (1956), *Nonparametric Statistics for the Behaviourial Sciences,* McGraw-Hill, Tokyo.

Singer, E., R. Gaefinkel, S.M. Cohen and L. Srole (1976), 'Mortality and mental health: evidence from the Midtown Manhatten Study', *Social Science and Medicine,* 10, 517-525.

Smith, J. (1987), 'Women at play: gender, the life-cycle and leisure', in J. Horne, D. Jary and A. Tomlinson, eds, *Sport, Leisure and Social Relations,* Routledge, London.

Sorenson, K.H. (1988), 'State of health and its association with death among old people at three years follow-up', *Danish Medical Bulletin,* 35, 597-600.

Sports Council (1982), *Sport in the Community: The Next Ten Years,* Sports Council, London.

Sports Council (1988), *Sport in the Community: into the 90s. A Strategy for Sport 1988-1993*, Sports Council, London.
Steptoe, A. (1990), 'The beneficial psychological effects of moderate aerobic exercise on adults from the general population', in *Fit for Life*. Health Promotion Research Trust, Cambridge.
Stewart, A.L. (1982), 'The reliability and validity of self-reported weight and height', *Journal of Chronic Diseases*, 35, 295-309.
Stewart, A.W., R.T. Jackson, M.A. Ford and R. Beaglehole (1987), 'Underestimation of relative weight by use of self-reported height and weight', *American Journal of Epidemiology*, 125, 122-126.
Suchman, E.A., B.S. Phillips and G.F. Streib (1958), 'An analysis of the validity of health questionnaires', *Social Forces*, 36, 223-232.
Thompson, S.M. (1990), 'Thank the ladies for the plates: the incorporation of women into sport', *Leisure Studies*, 9, 135-143.
Tomlinson, M. and D. Walton (1986), 'A sporting chance', *Leisure Management*, 6, 41-42.
Tornstam, L. (1975), 'Health and self-perception: a systems theoretical approach', *Gerontologist*, 15, 264-270.
Townsend, P., N. Davidson and M. Whitehead (1988), *Inequalities in Health*, Penguin, London.
Tregoning, D., N. Gent and D. Stephenson (1990), 'A comparison of the response of manual and non-manual workers to fitness testing', *Health Education Journal*, 49, 1, 30-31.
Veal, A.J. (1985), *Using Sports Centres*, Polytechnic of North London.
Veal, A.J. (1989), 'Leisure and life-style: a pluralist framework for analysis', *Leisure Studies*, 8, 141-153.
Wan, T.T.H. (1976), 'Predicting self-assessed health status: a multivariate approach', *Health Services Research*, 11, 464-477.
Wilson, C.C. and F.E. Netting (1987), 'Comparison of self and health professionals' ratings of the health of community-based elderly', *International Journal of Ageing and Human Development*, 25, 1, 11-25.
Wimbush, E. and M. Talbot, eds (1988), *Relative Freedoms*, Open University Press, Milton Keynes.
World Health Organization Expert Committee (1978), *Arterial Hypertension*, Technical Report Series No. 628, Geneva.
Wynne, D. (1990), 'Leisure, lifestyle and the construction of social position', *Leisure Studies*, 9, 21-34.
York, C., S. Dench, J. Minten and K. Roberts (1989), 'Indoor sport provisions and participants', in B.J.H. Brown, ed, *Leisure and the Environment*, Leisure Studies Association Conference Papers 31, Eastbourne, 58-77.